THE LEADER OF TOMORROW

Essential Qualities for Future Success

Wayne E. Smith

"In a rapidly changing world, the most effective leaders are those who can adapt, innovate, and stay ahead of the curve."

— John C. Maxwell

Contents

Preface

In an age characterized by unprecedented technological advancement, globalization, and evolving social norms, leadership is being redefined at an accelerated pace. As we navigate this transformative era, it becomes increasingly apparent that traditional notions of leadership are no longer sufficient. Future leaders must possess new qualities and skills to effectively address the complexities and opportunities of a rapidly changing world.

The Leader of Tomorrow: Essential Qualities for Future Success emerges from the need to understand and adapt to these shifting paradigms. This book is born from the conviction that the essence of leadership is not static but evolves in response to the forces that shape our world. Whether you are an aspiring leader, a seasoned executive, or someone with a vested interest in leadership dynamics, this book aims to provide valuable insights into what it means to lead in the future.

As we delve into the chapters, we will explore how technological innovations such as artificial intelligence and data analytics reshape decision-making processes and leadership roles. We will examine the impact of globalization on leadership strategies and the necessity for cultural competency in an interconnected world. Moreover, we will address how shifting social norms redefine expectations, focusing on ethical leadership, emotional intelligence, and inclusivity.

The purpose of this book is not merely to analyze the trends but to offer a practical guide to developing the qualities that will enable leaders to thrive amidst these changes. By identifying essential traits such as adaptability, resilience, and strategic vision, we aim to equip you with the tools to lead effectively and ethically in the face of uncertainty.

I have drawn from various sources in crafting this book, including contemporary research, case studies, and personal observations. I aim to present a comprehensive and actionable framework to help you navigate the evolving leadership landscape and inspire positive change.

As you embark on this journey through the pages of *The Leader of Tomorrow*, please reflect on your leadership aspirations and consider how you can cultivate the qualities necessary for future success. Together, let us explore what it takes to lead with integrity, innovation, and empathy in a world that demands nothing less.

Welcome to a new era of leadership.

— Wayne E. Smith

1

Redefining Leadership for the Future

Introduction to Future Leadership:

Evolving Definition and Expectations of Leadership

Expanding Beyond Traditional Leadership Models

Historical Context: Traditionally, leadership was often defined by authoritative figures with a top-down approach. Leaders were seen as decision-makers and directors, primarily focusing on control and direction.

Modern Shift: Today's leadership models are increasingly collaborative and inclusive. The emphasis shifts towards shared leadership and empowerment, where leaders facilitate and support rather than dictate.

This reflects a broader societal move towards democratization and flattening of organizational hierarchies.

Emphasis on Emotional Intelligence and Empathy

Traditional Traits: Historically, leadership was often associated with decisiveness, assertiveness, and strategic thinking. Emotional intelligence (EQ) was less emphasized, and leaders were frequently expected to maintain a professional distance from their teams.

Current Trends: Modern leadership strongly emphasizes emotional intelligence, including empathy, self-awareness, and relational skills. Leaders are now expected to understand and respond to their teams' emotional needs, build trust, and foster a supportive work environment. This shift acknowledges the importance of human connection in achieving organizational success and well-being.

Adapting to Technological and Global Changes

Past Paradigms: Leadership definitions once centered around managing people and resources in a relatively stable environment. The focus was primarily on operational efficiency and incremental improvements.

Emerging Expectations: Today's leaders must navigate rapid technological advancements and globalization. This includes understanding and leveraging digital tools, managing remote and diverse teams, and addressing global challenges such as climate change and geopolitical tensions. Leaders are expected to be agile, tech-savvy, and globally minded, capable of guiding organizations through complex and rapidly changing landscapes.

Increased Focus on Ethical Leadership and Social Responsibility

Historical Norms: In the past, leadership often prioritized organizational performance and profit maximization, sometimes at the expense of ethical considerations and social impact.

Current Emphasis: Modern leadership emphasizes ethical behavior, transparency, and corporate social responsibility. Leaders are increasingly held accountable for their organizations' social and environmental impacts. This shift reflects growing public expectations for businesses to contribute positively to society and operate with integrity.

Leadership as a Facilitator of Innovation and Creativity

Traditional Views: Leadership was once seen as primarily about maintaining order and efficiency, focusing less on fostering creativity or innovation.

Contemporary Role: Today's leaders are expected to be catalysts for innovation and creativity. They create environments where new ideas can flourish, encourage risk-taking, and support continuous learning and improvement. This role involves managing existing processes and inspiring and driving transformative change.

Emphasis on Lifelong Learning and Adaptability

Historical Perspective: Leadership roles were traditionally associated with a specific set of skills and knowledge that, once acquired, were expected to remain relevant throughout one's career.

Modern Approach: The fast pace of change in today's world means that leaders must engage in lifelong learning and adaptability. The ability to continuously update skills, embrace new knowledge, and adjust strategies is crucial for staying adequate and relevant in a dynamic environment.

Conclusion

The definition and expectations of leadership are evolving from a static and hierarchical model to a dynamic and inclusive one. Leaders are now expected to be empathetic, technologically adept, ethically grounded, and capable of fostering innovation and adaptability. This evolution reflects broader societal changes and the need for leadership that can navigate complexity and drive positive change in an increasingly interconnected world.

Key Drivers of Change:

Technological Advancements Impact on Leadership:

Increased Efficiency and Data-Driven Decision-Making:

Technology: The rise of big data, artificial intelligence (AI), and machine learning has revolutionized how leaders make decisions. Leaders can now access vast amounts of data and use advanced analytics to drive strategic decisions.

Leadership Impact: This shift has made leaders more reliant on data-driven insights, demanding skills in interpreting complex data and making informed decisions based on real-time information. It also emphasizes the need for leaders to stay updated with technological trends and innovations.

Remote Work and Digital Communication:

Technology: Tools like Zoom, Microsoft Teams, and Slack have made remote work feasible and transformed organizational communication.

Leadership Impact: Leaders must now manage dispersed teams, requiring virtual team management and digital communication skills. This also demands a greater focus on maintaining team cohesion and morale in a virtual environment.

Automation and Efficiency:

Technology: Automation technologies streamline repetitive tasks and processes, allowing organizations to increase efficiency.

Leadership Impact: Leaders need to navigate the implications of automation on the workforce, including reskilling employees and addressing concerns about job displacement.

Globalization

Impact on Leadership:

Cultural Competence and Diversity:

Globalization: The interconnectedness of global markets means that organizations often operate across different cultural and geographic regions.

Leadership Impact: Leaders must develop cultural competence to manage diverse teams and understand global markets effectively. This includes fostering inclusivity and addressing the challenges of

cross-cultural communication.

Global Supply Chains and Market Expansion:

Globalization: Organizations are increasingly involved in complex global supply chains and exploring international markets.

Leadership Impact: Leaders must navigate the complexities of global supply chains, including managing international partners and addressing geopolitical risks. They also need strategies for expanding and competing in global markets.

Global Challenges and Opportunities:

Globalization: Climate change, economic instability, and global health crises impact organizations worldwide.

Leadership Impact: Leaders must address these global challenges through sustainable practices and corporate social responsibility and be adept at seizing global opportunities for innovation and growth.

Shifting Social Norms

Impact on Leadership:

Increased Emphasis on Ethical Leadership and Social Responsibility:

Social Norms: There is a growing public demand for organizations to operate ethically and contribute positively to society.

Leadership Impact: Leaders are increasingly held accountable for their organization's social and environmental impact. They must incorporate ethical considerations into decision-making and promote corporate social responsibility.

Focus on Employee Well-Being and Work-Life Balance:

Social Norms: A greater emphasis is on work-life balance and employee well-being.

Leadership Impact: Leaders must create supportive work environments prioritizing employee well-being, mental health, and work-life balance. This includes implementing policies that support flexible working arrangements and a healthy work culture.

Advocacy for Diversity, Equity, and Inclusion (DEI):

Social Norms: There is an increasing focus on diversity, equity, and inclusion within organizations.

Leadership Impact: Leaders are tasked with fostering a diverse and inclusive workplace. This involves addressing systemic biases, implementing DEI initiatives, and ensuring equitable employee opportunities.

Conclusion

Technological advancements, globalization, and shifting social norms reshape the leadership landscape. Leaders must adapt to the increased reliance on technology and data, manage the complexities of global operations, and respond to evolving social expectations regarding ethics, diversity, and employee

well-being. The ability to navigate these changes effectively is crucial for modern leaders to drive organizational success and positive impact in a rapidly changing world.

Future Leadership Traits:

To thrive in the future, leaders must cultivate essential qualities that address the evolving demands of a rapidly changing world. Here are some of the essential qualities:

Adaptability and Flexibility

Description: The ability to adjust strategies and approaches to new information, changing conditions, or unexpected challenges.

Importance: As technology, markets, and social norms evolve, leaders must be agile and open to change to keep their organizations competitive and resilient.

Technological Proficiency

Description: A strong understanding of emerging technologies, data analytics, and digital tools.

Importance: Leaders must leverage technology to drive innovation, optimize operations, and make data-driven decisions.

Emotional Intelligence

Description: The capacity to understand and manage one's own emotions and the emotions of others.

Importance: High emotional intelligence enables leaders to build strong relationships, navigate complex interpersonal dynamics, and foster a positive work environment.

Cultural Competence

Description: The ability to interact effectively with people from diverse cultural backgrounds.

Importance: As globalization increases, leaders must be adept at managing multicultural teams and understanding global markets.

Ethical Integrity

Description: A commitment to acting with honesty, fairness, and responsibility.

Importance: Leaders are expected to uphold high ethical standards and promote corporate social responsibility, addressing societal and environmental concerns.

Strategic Vision

Description: The ability to foresee future trends, set long-term goals, and develop strategic plans.

Importance: A clear strategic vision helps leaders guide their organizations toward future success and navigate long-term challenges.

Resilience and Stress Management

Description: The capacity to remain focused and effective under pressure and recover from setbacks.

Importance: Leaders must handle stress, bounce back from failures, and maintain performance during challenging times.

Inclusive Leadership

Description: A commitment to creating a diverse and inclusive environment where all employees feel valued and have equal opportunities.

Importance: Inclusive leadership fosters innovation, engagement, and better decision-making by leveraging diverse perspectives.

Collaboration and Team Building

Description: The ability to work effectively with others, build strong teams, and foster a collaborative work culture.

Importance: Effective collaboration drives innovation, improves problem-solving, and enhances team performance.

Lifelong Learning and Curiosity

Description: A continuous desire to learn and grow, keeping up with new knowledge and skills.

Importance: Leaders committed to lifelong learning stay ahead of industry trends, adapt to changes, and drive personal and organizational growth.

Conclusion

Future leaders will need a blend of adaptability, technological savvy, emotional intelligence, and ethical integrity to navigate an increasingly complex and dynamic world. By cultivating these essential qualities, leaders can effectively steer their organizations through the challenges and opportunities that lie ahead.

2

Embracing Technological Advancements

Technological Integration:

Emerging technologies such as artificial intelligence (AI), automation, and other digital innovations are profoundly shaping the future of leadership. Here's an examination of how these technologies will influence leadership roles and practices:

Enhanced Decision-Making: Leaders will increasingly rely on AI and data analytics to make informed decisions. These technologies can rapidly analyze vast amounts of data, providing valuable insights and forecasts that guide strategic planning. AI-driven tools will help leaders identify trends, predict outcomes, and base decisions on evidence rather than intuition alone.

Greater Focus on Emotional Intelligence: As AI and automation handle routine tasks, leaders must focus more on areas where human qualities excel, such as emotional intelligence, empathy, and interpersonal skills. Effective leadership involves managing and motivating teams, understanding employee needs, and creating a supportive work environment—skills AI cannot replicate.

Shift in Leadership Skills: Future leaders will need solid technological literacy to integrate and manage emerging technologies effectively. Understanding AI, automation, and digital tools will be essential for leveraging these technologies' potential and remaining competitive.

Reshaping Organizational Structures: Automation and AI may lead to flatter organizational structures by reducing the need for middle management roles. Leaders must focus on creating more agile and flexible organizations that can quickly adapt to technological changes and market demands.

Ethical and Social Implications: Using AI and automation raises ethical considerations, such as data privacy, algorithmic bias, and job displacement. Leaders must navigate these challenges responsibly, ensuring that technology is used ethically and its benefits are distributed equitably.

Transformation of Workplaces: Emerging technologies facilitate remote and hybrid work arrangements, impacting leadership styles and practices. Leaders must manage distributed teams effectively, leveraging technology to maintain communication, collaboration, and engagement across various locations.

Accelerated Innovation: As technology evolves rapidly, leaders must foster a culture of continuous innovation. This involves encouraging creativity, supporting experimentation, and staying ahead of technological trends to drive organizational growth and competitiveness.

Enhanced Personalization: AI can provide personalized leadership development programs, tailoring training and development opportunities to individual needs and preferences. This customization will allow leaders to develop skills and competencies that align with their unique strengths and career goals.

Collaboration and Networking: Technology enables leaders to collaborate and network globally, accessing diverse perspectives and expertise. While this connectivity enhances problem-solving and innovation, leaders must navigate cultural and communication differences effectively.

Focus on Continuous Learning: With the rapid pace of technological change, leaders must engage in lifelong learning to stay updated on emerging trends and technologies. Continuous education and adaptability will be crucial for maintaining leadership effectiveness in an evolving technological landscape.

Digital Leadership Skills:

To manage and leverage technology effectively, leaders and professionals must cultivate various skills to harness technological advancements for organizational growth and efficiency. Here are some essential skills required:

Technological Literacy:

Understanding Core Technologies: Proficiency in core technologies such as artificial intelligence, data analytics, and automation is essential. Leaders need to understand these technologies' functions, potential, and limitations to make informed decisions about their implementation.

Keeping Up with Trends: Staying current with technological trends and emerging tools helps leaders anticipate changes and adapt strategies accordingly.

Data Analysis and Interpretation:

Data-Driven Decision Making: The ability to analyze and interpret data is crucial for making informed decisions. Leaders should be skilled in using data analytics tools to extract meaningful insights from large datasets and apply these insights to strategic planning.

Understanding Metrics: Proficiency in interpreting key performance indicators (KPIs) and other relevant metrics helps assess the effectiveness of technological solutions and their impact on business objectives.

Cybersecurity Awareness:

Protecting Digital Assets: Understanding cybersecurity principles is vital for safeguarding organizational data and infrastructure. Leaders should be aware of potential threats and ensure robust security measures are in place to protect against data breaches and cyber-attacks.

Compliance and Risk Management: Familiarity with regulations and best practices for data protection helps manage risks and maintain compliance with legal requirements.

Change Management:

Leading Technology Adoption: Effective change management skills are essential for guiding teams through adopting new technologies. Leaders must communicate the benefits of technological changes, address resistance, and ensure a smooth transition.

Training and Support: Adequate employee training and support help overcome the learning curves associated with new technologies and maximize their utilization.

Innovation and Problem Solving:

Encouraging Creativity: Fostering a culture of innovation involves encouraging creativity and experimentation with new technologies. Leaders should support initiatives that explore innovative applications and solutions.

Strategic Problem Solving: The ability to identify technological challenges and develop strategic solutions is crucial for effectively leveraging technology. Leaders must be adept at troubleshooting and resolving issues arising from technology integration.

Communication Skills:

Translating Technical Information: Effective communication skills are needed to translate complex technical information into understandable terms for stakeholders needing a technical background. This helps in aligning technology initiatives with organizational goals.

Collaborating Across Teams: Coordinating with various departments and teams ensures that technological solutions are implemented effectively and meet the needs of all stakeholders.

Project Management:

Managing Technology Projects: To oversee technology implementations, strong project management skills are required. This includes planning, budgeting, and managing resources to ensure that projects are completed on time and within scope.

Evaluating Outcomes: Assessing the success of technology projects involves evaluating outcomes against objectives and making adjustments as needed to optimize results.

Adaptability and Continuous Learning:

Embracing Change: The technology landscape is constantly evolving, so leaders must be adaptable and open to learning new skills and tools. Continuous learning ensures that leaders remain effective in managing and leveraging new technologies.

Agility in Response: Quickly adapting to technological changes and market demands is crucial for maintaining a competitive edge.

By developing these skills, leaders and professionals can effectively manage and leverage technology, driving innovation and enhancing organizational performance.

Case Studies:

Satya Nadella – Microsoft

Satya Nadella became CEO of Microsoft in 2014, during a time when the company faced significant challenges amid rapid technological evolution. Under his leadership, Microsoft shifted its focus toward cloud computing and artificial intelligence, moving away from its traditional software business. The launch of Azure, Microsoft's cloud platform, was a major success and positioned the company as a leading player in the cloud market. This strategic pivot revitalized Microsoft, resulting in significant growth in stock value and market share.

Elon Musk – Tesla and SpaceX

Elon Musk, CEO of Tesla and SpaceX, is known for pushing technological boundaries in the automotive and aerospace industries. His leadership involved aggressive investments in electric vehicles and space technology. Tesla's advancements in electric vehicles and autonomous driving technology revolutionized the automotive industry, while SpaceX achieved cost-effective space travel with reusable rockets. Musk's innovations have significantly impacted both sectors, establishing Tesla as a leader in clean energy and SpaceX as a prominent aerospace company.

Jeff Bezos – Amazon

Jeff Bezos founded Amazon in 1994 as an online bookstore and transformed it into one of the largest technology and e-commerce companies in the world. His leadership expanded Amazon's offerings beyond books to a wide array of products and services. Bezos also spearheaded the development of Amazon Web Services (AWS), which has become a major force in cloud computing. Amazon's success as a global retail and cloud computing giant is a testament to Bezos's strategic vision and ability to navigate technological changes.

Sheryl Sandberg – Facebook (Meta)

Sheryl Sandberg joined Facebook (now Meta) as Chief Operating Officer in 2008, contributing to its transformation from a college networking site into a global social media leader. Sandberg played a crucial role in developing Facebook's advertising model, which significantly boosted revenue. She also focused on expanding the platform's capabilities and integrating new technologies to enhance user engagement. Her leadership helped solidify Facebook's position as one of the most influential social media platforms.

Sundar Pichai – Google (Alphabet Inc.)

Sundar Pichai became CEO of Google in 2015 and later CEO of its parent company, Alphabet Inc., in 2019. Pichai emphasized the development of artificial intelligence and machine learning technologies, leading initiatives such as Google Assistant and advancements in AI-driven search algorithms. Under his guidance, Google has maintained its position as a leading technology company, with significant progress in AI and machine learning driving growth and keeping the company at the forefront of technological developments.

3

Navigating a Globalized World

Cultural Competency:

Understanding and managing diverse teams is crucial for organizational success in today's globalized and interconnected world. Here are key reasons why this skill is essential:

Enhanced Creativity and Innovation

Diverse teams bring together various perspectives, experiences, and problem-solving approaches. This variety fosters creativity and innovation, as team members can approach challenges from different angles and offer unique solutions. Research has shown that diverse teams are better at generating innovative ideas and finding creative solutions to complex problems.

Improved Problem-Solving

With a mix of backgrounds and viewpoints, diverse teams can address problems more comprehensively. They are less likely to suffer from groupthink, which often limits creativity and effective problem-solving. Team members' diverse experiences contribute to a broader understanding of issues, leading to more effective and well-rounded solutions.

Better Decision-Making

Diverse teams can make more informed and balanced decisions. By incorporating multiple perspectives, these teams are better equipped to evaluate various aspects of a situation and consider a broader range of potential outcomes. This comprehensive approach can lead to more robust and effective decision-making processes.

Increased Employee Engagement and Satisfaction

Employees who feel that their identities and contributions are valued are likelier to be engaged and satisfied with their work. A culture of inclusivity and respect fosters a positive work environment where all team members feel motivated to contribute their best. This can lead to higher retention rates and a more committed workforce.

Enhanced Customer Insights

A diverse team can better understand and address the needs of a diverse customer base. Team members who reflect the demographics of customers can provide insights into preferences, behaviors, and expectations, leading to products and services that better meet the needs of a varied market.

Improved Communication and Collaboration

Understanding and managing diverse teams requires effective communication and collaboration skills. Leaders must be adept at navigating cultural differences, managing conflicts, and fostering an environment where all voices are heard. This not only improves team dynamics but also enhances overall productivity and cohesion.

Strengthened Organizational Reputation

Organizations that embrace and effectively manage diversity are often viewed more favorably by clients, customers, and potential employees. A commitment to diversity and inclusion can enhance a company's reputation as a forward-thinking and socially responsible organization, attracting talent and building customer loyalty.

Compliance with Legal and Ethical Standards

Understanding and managing diverse teams is essential for compliance with legal and ethical standards regarding workplace discrimination and equality. Effective diversity management helps organizations avoid legal issues and demonstrates a commitment to fair and equitable employee treatment.

Global Challenges:

In the future, leaders will confront various global issues that require effective management and strategic foresight. Here are critical global challenges and how leaders can address them:

Climate Change

Climate change significantly threatens global stability, impacting ecosystems, economies, and human health. Leaders must champion and implement sustainable practices, promote green technologies, and foster international cooperation to mitigate environmental damage. Effective leadership in this area involves setting ambitious goals for reducing carbon emissions and investing in adaptation strategies to cope with the impacts of climate change.

International Conflicts

Ongoing and emerging international conflicts, driven by geopolitical tensions, resource scarcity, and ideological differences, will require leaders to navigate complex diplomatic landscapes. Leaders must employ conflict resolution and negotiation skills to address disputes, promote peace, and build alliances. Understanding the root causes of conflicts and engaging in multilateral dialogue will be essential for maintaining global stability.

Economic Inequality

Economic inequality within and between nations remains a pressing issue with far-reaching social and political implications. Leaders must address disparities in wealth and opportunity by implementing policies that promote economic inclusivity, access to education, and equitable growth. Collaborative efforts with international organizations and stakeholders will be crucial for creating sustainable financial solutions.

Pandemics and Health Crises

The COVID-19 pandemic highlighted the need for effective leadership in managing global health crises. Leaders must be prepared to handle future pandemics by strengthening public health systems, investing in research and development, and ensuring equitable access to healthcare resources. Coordinated global responses and robust health policies will be vital to mitigating the impacts of health emergencies.

Technological Disruptions

Rapid technological advancements, including artificial intelligence, automation, and cybersecurity threats, will shape the future of global leadership. Leaders will need to navigate the challenges and opportunities presented by these technologies, ensuring that they are harnessed for positive societal impact while managing risks such as job displacement and data privacy concerns.

Migration and Refugee Crises

Conflicts, environmental changes, and economic hardships drive global migration and refugee movements. Leaders must develop humane and effective policies for managing migration, protecting refugees, and addressing the root causes of displacement. Collaborative international approaches and support systems will be vital for addressing these complex issues.

Human Rights and Social Justice

Ensuring human rights and advancing social justice are fundamental challenges for global leaders. Addressing issues such as discrimination, inequality, and human rights abuses requires strong advocacy, policy reform, and international cooperation. Leaders must champion human rights and work towards creating a more equitable and just world.

Resource Management

The sustainable management of natural resources, including water, energy, and minerals, is critical for future stability. Leaders will need to balance economic development with environmental conservation, promoting responsible consumption and innovative solutions for resource management. International collaboration will be essential for addressing global resource challenges.

Education and Skills Development

As the global workforce evolves, leaders must prioritize education and skills development to prepare individuals for the future job market. Investing in education systems, lifelong learning opportunities, and skills training will be crucial for addressing workforce shifts and ensuring that individuals are equipped to thrive in a rapidly changing world.

Global Governance and Cooperation

Effective global governance and cooperation are essential for addressing transnational issues. Leaders must strengthen international institutions, foster collaboration among nations, and promote shared responsibilities for global challenges. Building consensus and working together on common goals will be vital to achieving sustainable and equitable outcomes

Building Global Networks:

Creating and maintaining international connections and collaborations are crucial for addressing global challenges, fostering innovation, and enhancing cross-cultural understanding. Here are effective strategies for building and sustaining these global relationships:

Establish Clear Objectives

Define the goals and outcomes of the international collaboration. Whether for business, research, or diplomatic purposes, having clear objectives helps align efforts and ensures all parties have a shared vision and purpose.

Build Strong Networks

Develop a broad and diverse network of international contacts. Attend global conferences, join international organizations, and participate in global forums to connect with potential collaborators and expand your network.

Leverage Technology

Utilize digital tools and platforms for communication and collaboration. Video conferencing, collaborative software, and social media can facilitate real-time interactions, making it easier to maintain connections and manage projects across different time zones.

Foster Mutual Understanding

Promote cultural competence and sensitivity by learning about your international partners' customs, values, and business practices. Understanding and respecting cultural differences can help build trust and prevent misunderstandings.

Develop Strong Communication Channels

Establish clear and open lines of communication. Regular updates, transparent discussions, and feedback mechanisms are essential for effective collaboration. Ensure that communication is adapted to accommodate language differences and time zone challenges.

Build Trust and Relationships

Invest time in developing personal relationships with international partners. Trust is a cornerstone of successful collaboration, and solid personal connections can enhance professional interactions and facilitate smoother negotiations.

Ensure Legal and Ethical Compliance

Be aware of and comply with international laws, regulations, and ethical standards. This includes understanding legal requirements for contracts, intellectual property, and data protection and adhering to ethical practices in business and research.

Create Shared Value

Focus on creating value for all parties involved. Identify mutual benefits and ensure that the collaboration is advantageous for each partner. This can help sustain long-term relationships and ensure continued engagement.

Establish Clear Roles and Responsibilities

Clearly define the roles, responsibilities, and expectations for each partner. Having well-defined roles helps prevent conflicts and ensures that each party knows their contributions and obligations.

Monitor and Evaluate Progress

Assess the collaboration's progress and outcomes regularly. Use metrics and feedback to evaluate the partnership's effectiveness and make necessary adjustments to improve performance and address any issues.

Promote Shared Goals and Values

Align collaboration with shared goals and values to strengthen the partnership. When all parties are committed to common objectives and values, cooperation enhances and ensures a unified approach.

Adapt to Changes

Be flexible and adaptable to changes in the global environment, including political, economic, and social shifts. Adapting to changes can help maintain relevance and effectiveness in international collaborations.

Encourage Innovation and Knowledge Sharing

Foster an environment that supports innovation and the sharing of knowledge. Encourage the exchange of ideas, best practices, and expertise to drive growth and advance the collaboration's goals.

Invest in Capacity Building

Support capacity-building initiatives to enhance partners' skills and capabilities. Training, workshops, and resource sharing can strengthen collaboration and contribute to long-term success.

Celebrate Successes and Milestones

Recognize and celebrate achievements and milestones in the collaboration. Celebrating successes helps build morale, reinforce positive relationships, and demonstrate appreciation for all partners' efforts.

4

Leading with Empathy and Emotional Intelligence

Emotional Intelligence in Leadership:

Emotional Intelligence (EI) refers to the ability to recognize, understand, manage, and effectively use one's own emotions and the emotions of others. It encompasses several key components:

Self-Awareness: Recognizing and understanding one's emotions and their impact on thoughts and behavior.

Self-Regulation: Managing and controlling one's emotions healthily and constructively.

Motivation: Harnessing emotions to stay focused on goals and persist in facing challenges.

Empathy: Understanding and being sensitive to the emotions and perspectives of others.

Social Skills: Effectively managing relationships, communicating clearly, and building strong, positive connections with others.

Significance in Leadership

Enhanced Communication: Leaders with high emotional intelligence can communicate more effectively by understanding and addressing their team members' emotions. This leads to clearer, more empathetic interactions and helps resolve conflicts constructively.

Improved Conflict Resolution: Emotionally intelligent leaders can address conflicts more effectively by recognizing and managing their own emotions and those of others. They can mediate disputes, negotiate solutions, and foster a harmonious work environment.

More robust Team Dynamics: Leaders with empathy and social skills can build stronger, more cohesive teams. They understand team members' needs and motivations, which enhances collaboration and boosts morale.

Increased Adaptability: Emotional intelligence allows leaders to remain composed and resilient in the face of change and uncertainty. They can adapt their leadership style to suit different situations and challenges, making them more effective in dynamic environments.

Enhanced Decision-Making: Leaders with high emotional intelligence are better equipped to make informed decisions by balancing emotional considerations with rational analysis. This leads to more thoughtful and well-rounded decision-making processes.

Better Employee Engagement and Satisfaction: Emotionally intelligent Leaders are likelier to create a supportive and positive work environment. This contributes to higher levels of employee engagement, satisfaction, and retention.

Leadership Effectiveness: Overall, emotional intelligence contributes to a leader's effectiveness by enabling them to manage their own emotions and understand the feelings of others. This fosters a positive organizational culture and drives better outcomes for the team and the organization.

Emotional intelligence is crucial for leadership because it enhances communication, conflict resolution, team dynamics, adaptability, decision-making, employee satisfaction, and overall leadership effectiveness. Leaders who develop and utilize emotional intelligence are better positioned to lead effectively and achieve organizational success.

Building Trust and Connection:

Strong relationships and trust within teams are essential for creating a collaborative, productive, and positive work environment. Here are several effective techniques for building and maintaining these crucial elements:

Open Communication

Encourage Transparency: Create an environment where team members feel comfortable sharing ideas, concerns, and feedback without fear of retribution. Communicate goals, changes, and expectations clearly and regularly.

Active Listening: Practice active listening by giving full attention to team members when they speak, asking clarifying questions, and summarizing their points to ensure understanding.

Build Rapport

Personal Connections: Take the time to get to know team members personally. Show genuine interest in their lives, celebrate milestones, and engage in casual conversations to strengthen relationships.

Team-Building Activities: Organize activities, allowing team members to interact outside work tasks. These can include team-building exercises, social events, or collaborative projects.

Show Empathy and Understanding

Acknowledge Emotions: Recognize and validate team members' feelings and perspectives. Empathy helps build trust and demonstrates that you value their experiences and viewpoints.

Provide Support: Offer support during challenging times, whether personal or professional. Be approachable and provide resources or assistance when needed.

Foster Collaboration

Encourage Teamwork: Promote a collaborative culture where team members work together towards common goals. Facilitate group discussions, brainstorming sessions, and joint problem-solving activities.

Share Credit and Success: Recognize and celebrate team achievements. Credit individuals and the team as a whole, fostering a sense of shared success and mutual respect.

Build Reliability and Integrity

Follow Through on Promises: Be consistent and deliver on commitments. Reliability builds trust and demonstrates that you are dependable and honest.

Demonstrate Ethical Behavior: Uphold high ethical standards and lead by example. Being transparent, fair, and respectful reinforces trust and sets a positive example for the team.

Promote Inclusivity and Respect

Value Diversity: Embrace and respect diverse perspectives and backgrounds within the team. Encourage an inclusive culture where all voices are heard and valued.

Address Conflicts Constructively: Handle conflicts fairly and respectfully. Address issues promptly and work towards mutually beneficial solutions.

Encourage Feedback and Growth

Provide Constructive Feedback: Offer regular, constructive feedback to help team members improve and grow. Ensure feedback is specific, actionable, and delivered with respect.

Support Professional Development: Invest in team members' development by providing opportunities for training, skill-building, and career growth.

Build a Positive Work Environment

Foster a Culture of Appreciation: Regularly express appreciation and gratitude for team members' contributions. Recognize their efforts and celebrate their successes.

Create a Supportive Atmosphere: Ensure the work environment is supportive and encouraging. Address any issues that may impact team morale and well-being.

Lead with Authenticity

Be Genuine: Demonstrate authenticity in your leadership style. Being honest and trustworthy to yourself builds trust and encourages team members to do the same.

Share Your Vision: Clearly articulate your vision and values for the team. Aligning actions with values helps build credibility and fosters a shared sense of purpose.

Encourage Accountability

Set Clear Expectations: Clearly define roles, responsibilities, and expectations. Ensure that team members understand their contributions to the team's goals.

Hold Everyone Accountable: Ensure that everyone, including yourself, is accountable for their actions and contributions. This promotes a sense of responsibility and trust within the team.

By implementing these techniques, leaders can foster strong relationships and trust within their teams, improving collaboration, productivity, and overall team success.

Empathy as a Leadership Tool:

Empathy is a powerful tool in leadership that can significantly enhance effectiveness by improving communication, fostering trust, and creating a positive work environment. Here are some notable case studies that illustrate how empathy enhances leadership effectiveness:

Satya Nadella at Microsoft

Case Study Overview: Satya Nadella became CEO of Microsoft in 2014, inheriting a company known for its competitive and siloed culture. Nadella's leadership approach focused on empathy, which he believed was crucial for transforming Microsoft's culture and improving overall performance.

Empathy in Action:

Cultural Transformation: Nadella emphasized the importance of understanding employees' perspectives and feelings, encouraging leaders to listen actively and respond to their needs. This shift fostered a more collaborative and inclusive work environment.

Growth Mindset: He promoted a "growth mindset" culture, where employees were encouraged to learn from failures rather than fearing them. By empathizing with employees' challenges, Nadella helped build resilience and a more innovative culture.

Outcome: Under Nadella's empathetic leadership, Microsoft experienced a significant cultural shift and saw improvements in employee satisfaction and engagement. The company also achieved remarkable financial success, notably increasing stock value and market performance.

Howard Schultz at Starbucks

Case Study Overview: Howard Schultz, the former CEO of Starbucks, is well-known for his empathetic leadership style. Schultz's approach was instrumental in shaping Starbucks' corporate culture and enhancing employee relations.

Empathy in Action:

Employee Benefits: Schultz implemented programs such as offering healthcare benefits to part-time employees, a rare practice in the retail industry. He believed understanding and addressing employees' needs were crucial for fostering loyalty and satisfaction.

Listening and Inclusion: Schultz actively sought employee feedback at all levels and included their perspectives in decision-making processes. This inclusive approach helped build community and trust within the organization.

Outcome: Schultz's empathetic leadership made Starbucks one of the most admired and successful global brands. The company enjoyed high employee retention rates and customer satisfaction, reinforcing the positive impact of empathy on organizational success.

Paul Polman at Unilever

Case Study Overview: Paul Polman, former CEO of Unilever, is recognized for emphasizing empathy and sustainability in leadership. Polman's leadership was marked by a commitment to creating positive social and environmental impacts while achieving business success.

Empathy in Action:

Sustainable Living Plan: Polman launched Unilever's Sustainable Living Plan, which aimed to improve the well-being of people and the planet. This initiative reflected empathy for global issues and the needs of communities affected by Unilever's operations.

Stakeholder Engagement: Polman focused on engaging with various stakeholders, including employees, customers, and suppliers, to understand their concerns and expectations. His empathetic approach helped align Unilever's business practices with broader societal goals.

Outcome: Under Polman's empathetic leadership, Unilever made significant strides in sustainability and corporate responsibility. The company saw improvements in brand reputation, customer loyalty, and financial performance, demonstrating the effectiveness of empathy-driven leadership in achieving long-term success.

Jacinda Ardern as Prime Minister of New Zealand

Case Study Overview: Jacinda Ardern, the Prime Minister of New Zealand, has been praised for her empathetic leadership, particularly in her response to crises and approach to governance.

Empathy in Action:

Response to the Christchurch Attacks: Ardern's compassionate and empathetic response to the Christchurch mosque shootings in 2019, including her swift action to address gun control and her supportive interactions with victims' families, showcased her deep understanding of the community's needs.

Inclusive Leadership: Ardern's leadership style emphasizes inclusivity and understanding. It addresses the diverse needs of New Zealand's population and fosters a sense of unity and support.

Outcome: Ardern's empathetic leadership has earned her widespread acclaim and respect domestically and internationally. Her approach has contributed to high levels of public trust and engagement, demonstrating the power of empathy in effective political leadership.

These case studies highlight how empathetic leadership can drive positive organizational change, enhance employee satisfaction, and contribute to overall success. By understanding and addressing the needs and concerns of others, leaders can build stronger, more effective teams and organizations.

5

Fostering Innovation and Creativity

Encouraging a Culture of Innovation:

Encouraging a culture of innovation within organizations involves creating an environment that fosters creativity, supports experimentation, and values new ideas. Here are strategies to promote creativity and drive innovation effectively:

Foster Open Communication

Strategy: Encourage open dialogue and transparent communication across all levels of the organization. **Implementation**: Create forums for employees to share ideas, feedback, and suggestions without fear of criticism. Regularly hold brainstorming sessions and innovation workshops where diverse perspectives can be heard and valued. **Impact**:

Open communication helps in surfacing innovative ideas from all levels of the organization and ensures that team members feel valued and heard.

Support Risk-Taking and Experimentation

Strategy: Create a safe environment for experimentation where taking calculated risks is encouraged. **Implementation**: Develop a framework for piloting new ideas and projects, and establish a "fail forward" mentality where failures are seen as learning opportunities rather than setbacks. Recognize and reward creative risk-taking. **Impact**: When employees are not afraid to fail, they are more likely to push boundaries and explore new solutions, leading to breakthroughs and innovative outcomes.

Encourage Continuous Learning

Strategy: Promote ongoing education and skills development. **Implementation**: Offer training programs, workshops, and access to educational resources that support skill development and knowledge expansion. Encourage employees to pursue learning opportunities that align with their interests and the organization's goals. **Impact**: Continuous learning helps employees stay updated with the latest trends and technologies, fostering a more innovative mindset.

Promote Cross-Functional Collaboration

Strategy: Facilitate collaboration between different departments and teams. **Implementation**: Create cross-functional teams for projects, encourage job rotation, and organize inter-departmental meetings to discuss challenges and opportunities. Use collaborative tools to streamline communication and project management. **Impact**: Diverse teams bring different perspectives and expertise, which can lead to more creative solutions and innovative approaches to problem-solving.

Recognize and Reward Innovation

Strategy: Implement recognition programs to celebrate and reward innovative contributions. **Implementation**: Develop awards or incentives for outstanding ideas and successful projects. Highlight achievements through company-wide communications and provide tangible rewards or recognition to motivate employees. **Impact**: Recognizing and rewarding innovation boosts morale and encourages employees to continue contributing creative ideas.

Provide Autonomy and Ownership

Strategy: Give employees the freedom to explore their ideas and take ownership of their projects.

Implementation: Allow team members to lead initiatives and make decisions related to their projects. Provide resources and support while giving them the autonomy to experiment and innovate.

Impact: Autonomy fosters a sense of ownership and accountability, motivating employees to invest more effort into their work and pursue innovative solutions.

Create a Stimulating Work Environment

Strategy: Design a work environment that inspires creativity and innovation.

Implementation: Use open office layouts, incorporate creative spaces such as lounges or brainstorming rooms, and provide tools and technologies that facilitate innovative work. Ensure the environment is conducive to both focused work and collaborative efforts. **Impact**: A stimulating work environment can enhance creativity by providing a setting that encourages new ideas and supports different working styles.

Lead by Example

Strategy: Demonstrate innovative thinking and a willingness to experiment at the leadership level.

Implementation: Leaders should actively participate in brainstorming sessions, share their own creative ideas, and support innovation initiatives. Show openness to new approaches and be willing to invest in innovative projects.

Impact: When leaders model innovative behavior, it sets a precedent for the rest of the organization and reinforces the importance of creativity in achieving organizational goals.

Encourage External Partnerships

Strategy: Collaborate with external partners to bring new perspectives and ideas.

Implementation: Establish partnerships with startups, research institutions, or other organizations to gain insights into emerging trends and technologies. Participate in industry events and innovation networks to stay connected with the broader ecosystem.

Impact: External partnerships can provide fresh perspectives, access to new technologies, and opportunities for collaborative innovation.

Monitor and Adapt to Trends

Strategy: Stay informed about industry trends and technological advancements.

Implementation: Regularly review market trends, emerging technologies, and competitive innovations. Adapt strategies and processes to incorporate relevant trends and maintain a competitive edge.

Impact: Monitoring trends ensures that the organization remains at the forefront of innovation and can adapt quickly to changes in the industry.

By implementing these strategies, organizations can create a culture that not only fosters creativity but also drives sustained innovation, leading to long-term success and competitive advantage.

Risk Management:

Introduction

Balancing risk and innovation is crucial for organizations aiming to achieve growth while mitigating potential pitfalls. Effective risk management ensures that innovative endeavors are pursued with a clear understanding of possible threats, enabling organizations to navigate uncertainties while capitalizing on opportunities. This balance requires a strategic approach integrating risk assessment with creative thinking and decision-making.

Understanding Risk and Innovation

Definition of Risk: Risk refers to the potential for loss or harm arising from uncertainty in decision-making. It encompasses various financial, operational, strategic, and reputational risks.

Definition of Innovation: Innovation involves introducing new ideas, products, or processes that provide value and drive progress. It often requires experimentation and exploration of uncharted territories, which inherently carries risk.

Importance of Balance: Balancing risk and innovation is essential because while innovation can drive growth and competitive advantage, it can also lead to failures if not appropriately managed. Effective risk management helps in navigating these challenges while encouraging creativity.

Establishing a Risk Management Framework

Risk Identification: Begin by identifying potential risks associated with innovative projects. This includes assessing market, technical, financial, and operational risks. SWOT analysis (Strengths, Weaknesses, Opportunities, Threats) and risk assessments can help identify these risks.

Risk Assessment: Evaluate the likelihood and impact of identified risks. Use qualitative and quantitative methods to prioritize risks based on their potential effect on the organization. This involves creating risk matrices and scenario planning to understand the implications of different risk levels.

Risk Mitigation Strategies: Develop strategies to mitigate identified risks. This could involve diversifying investments, implementing contingency plans, and using risk transfer mechanisms like insurance. Create a risk management plan that outlines how risks will be monitored and addressed.

Integrating Innovation with Risk Management

Encouraging Innovation: Foster a culture that supports innovation by providing resources, encouraging experimentation, and recognizing creative efforts. Develop frameworks that allow for controlled experimentation and pilot testing of new ideas.

Risk Tolerance and Appetite: Define the organization's risk tolerance and appetite. This involves understanding how much risk the organization will take to pursue innovation. Communicate these boundaries to teams to ensure alignment between risk management and innovation efforts.

Decision-Making Processes: Implement decision-making processes that integrate risk and innovation considerations. Use risk-adjusted return on investment (ROI) and scenario analysis tools to evaluate potential outcomes and make informed decisions.

Monitoring and Adjusting

Continuous Monitoring: Regularly monitor risks associated with innovative projects. Use key performance indicators (KPIs) and risk metrics to track progress and identify emerging issues.

Feedback Loops:

Establish feedback loops to learn from both successes and failures. Analyze outcomes to understand what worked, what didn't, and why.

Use these insights to adjust risk management strategies and innovation processes.

Adaptive Strategies: Be prepared to adapt strategies based on new information and changing circumstances. Flexibility allows organizations to respond to unforeseen risks and capitalize on new opportunities.

Case Studies and Examples

Example 1: Technology Startups: Many technology startups embrace high levels of risk in their pursuit of innovation. Companies like Tesla and SpaceX have successfully balanced risk and innovation by investing heavily in research and development while implementing robust risk management practices to address technological and market uncertainties.

Example 2: Pharmaceuticals: The pharmaceutical industry often faces high risks with drug development, including regulatory challenges and financial investments. Companies use stage-gate processes and clinical trials to manage risks while pursuing innovative treatments.

Conclusion

Balancing risk and innovation is a dynamic process that requires careful planning, strategic thinking, and ongoing management. By understanding and managing risks while fostering a culture of innovation, organizations can pursue new opportunities with confidence and resilience. Effective risk management ensures that innovative efforts are aligned with organizational goals and capabilities, leading to sustainable growth and success.

Success Stories:

Examples of Leaders Who Have Successfully Led Innovative Initiatives Introduction

Innovative leadership drives progress and transformation across industries. Successful leaders in innovative initiatives often blend creativity with strategic thinking to achieve remarkable results. Their stories provide valuable lessons on navigating challenges, inspiring teams, and bringing groundbreaking ideas to fruition. Here are some notable examples of leaders who have excelled in leading innovative initiatives.

Elon Musk – Tesla and SpaceX

Tesla, Inc.: Elon Musk, the CEO and founder of Tesla, has been a transformative force in the automotive industry. Under his leadership, Tesla revolutionized electric vehicles by making them desirable and practical. Musk's focus on innovation led to developing high-performance electric cars with long ranges and cutting-edge technology. Tesla's advancements in battery technology and autonomous driving have set new standards in the industry.

SpaceX: Musk's other major venture, SpaceX, has made significant strides in space exploration. The company has achieved milestones such as developing reusable rockets and successful missions to the

International Space Station. SpaceX's innovations in space technology, including the Falcon Heavy rocket and the Starship spacecraft, have redefined the possibilities of space travel and exploration.

Satya Nadella – Microsoft

Cloud Computing and AI: Satya Nadella, CEO of Microsoft, has been instrumental in transforming the company's approach to technology. Since taking the helm in 2014, Nadella has shifted Microsoft's focus towards cloud computing and artificial intelligence. Under his leadership, Microsoft Azure has become a leading cloud platform, driving growth and enabling businesses worldwide to leverage cloud services.

Cultural Transformation: Nadella's emphasis on fostering a growth mindset and inclusive culture has also been crucial. He has revitalized Microsoft's work environment by encouraging innovation and collaboration, increasing employee engagement and creativity. This cultural shift has played a vital role in the company's successful adaptation to the digital age.

Jeff Bezos – Amazon

E-commerce and Cloud Services: Jeff Bezos, the founder of Amazon, has pioneered e-commerce and cloud computing. Amazon's innovation in online retail transformed how consumers shop, leading to the widespread adoption of online purchasing. Bezos's vision for expanding Amazon's offerings led to the creation of Amazon Web Services

(AWS), a leading cloud computing platform that has revolutionized IT infrastructure for businesses globally.

Customer-Centric Approach: Bezos's relentless focus on customer satisfaction and operational efficiency has driven Amazon's success. His innovative initiatives, such as the development of Prime membership, Alexa, and drone delivery concepts, have continually set new benchmarks in the industry and shaped the future of retail and technology.

Indra Nooyi – PepsiCo

Sustainability and Healthier Products: Indra Nooyi, former CEO of PepsiCo, championed innovation in product development and sustainability. Under her leadership, PepsiCo shifted towards offering healthier food and beverage options, responding to changing consumer preferences and health trends.

Nooyi's emphasis on environmental sustainability led to initiatives to reduce PepsiCo's carbon footprint and improve water conservation.

Performance with Purpose: Nooyi's "Performance with Purpose" strategy integrated social and environmental goals with business performance. This approach advanced PepsiCo's market position and demonstrated how innovative leadership can align business objectives with broader societal impacts.

Tim Cook – Apple

Product Innovation: Tim Cook, CEO of Apple, has continued to drive innovation following Steve Jobs's tenure. Under Cook's leadership, Apple has introduced new product categories, such as the Apple Watch and AirPods, which have achieved significant market success. Cook's focus on integrating hardware, software, and services has enhanced the user experience and solidified Apple's position as a leader in consumer technology.

Sustainability Initiatives: Cook has also emphasized sustainability, guiding Apple towards a more environmentally responsible future. Apple's commitment to using 100% renewable energy for its global facilities and its efforts to reduce the environmental impact of its products reflect Cook's innovative approach to integrating technology with environmental stewardship.

Conclusion

These leaders exemplify how innovative thinking, strategic vision, and effective execution can drive transformative change. Their success stories illustrate the importance of balancing creativity with practical considerations, fostering a culture of innovation, and continually adapting to evolving challenges. By studying these examples, future leaders can gain insights into leading successful innovative initiatives and making a lasting impact in their respective fields.

6

Ethical Leadership and Social Responsibility

Ethical Decision-Making:

Frameworks for Making Ethical Choices in Leadership Introduction

E thical decision-making in leadership is crucial for maintaining integrity, fostering trust, and ensuring long-term success. Leaders are often faced with complex situations that require balancing various interests, values, and obligations. Understanding and applying ethical frameworks can help leaders navigate these challenges and make decisions that align with ethical principles. This exploration delves into several frameworks for ethical decision-making in leadership.

Utilitarianism

Utilitarianism is a consequentialist framework that focuses on decision outcomes. According to this approach, the ethical choice is the one that maximizes overall happiness or well-being and minimizes harm. Leaders using this framework assess the potential consequences of their decisions for all stakeholders and choose the option that produces the greatest net benefit.

Example: A company deciding whether to cut costs by reducing employee benefits might use utilitarianism to weigh the overall impact on employees, customers, and shareholders. The decision would aim to maximize benefits across all these groups, even if it involves some sacrifice from individual stakeholders.

Deontological Ethics

Deontological ethics emphasizes the importance of following moral rules or duties regardless of the outcomes. This framework is grounded in honesty, fairness, and respect for individuals' rights. Leaders applying deontological ethics focus on adhering to ethical principles and fulfilling their obligations, even if doing so does not lead to the best overall consequences.

Example: A leader who discovers that a financial report contains inaccuracies might choose to correct the errors and report them transparently, even if it leads to short-term financial losses or damage to the company's reputation. The commitment to truthfulness and integrity guides the decision.

Virtue Ethics

Virtue ethics centers on the character and virtues of the decision-maker rather than the consequences or rules. According to this framework, ethical decisions reflect virtuous traits such as courage, compassion, and justice. Leaders using virtue ethics consider how their choices align with their values and the character they aspire to cultivate.

Example: A leader facing a dilemma about promoting a less experienced employee over a more qualified candidate might base their decision on virtues like fairness and support for growth. The leader's choice would reflect their commitment to nurturing potential and fostering a positive work environment.

Ethical Relativism

Ethical relativism posits that moral standards and judgments are relative to cultural, social, or individual perspectives. Leaders employing this framework recognize that ethical norms can vary across contexts and strive to make decisions that respect these diverse viewpoints. Ethical relativism emphasizes understanding and adapting to the values of various stakeholders.

Example: In a global company operating in diverse cultural environments, a leader might navigate ethical decisions by considering local customs and practices while striving to uphold core ethical standards. This approach requires sensitivity to cultural differences and a commitment to balancing respect for local values with universal moral principles.

Justice Theory

Justice theory focuses on fairness and equality in decision-making. This framework emphasizes distributing benefits and burdens equitably among all affected parties. Leaders using justice theory strive to ensure that their decisions do not disproportionately favor or disadvantage any particular group and that they promote fairness and equality.

Example: A leader in a company implementing a new compensation system might use justice theory to design a structure that fairly rewards employees based on their performance and contributions. This would ensure that all employees are treated equitably and that compensation decisions are made transparently.

Care Ethics

Care ethics prioritize relationships and care and concern for others. This framework emphasizes empathy, compassion, and the responsibility to support and nurture others. Leaders who apply care ethics focus on the well-being of individuals and the impact of their decisions on personal relationships and the community.

Example: A leader who faces a decision about downsizing might choose to implement measures that support affected employees, such as providing severance packages and career counseling. This decision reflects a commitment to caring for the individuals impacted by the decision and supporting their transition.

Conclusion

Ethical decision-making in leadership requires a thoughtful application of various frameworks to navigate complex and often conflicting values and interests. By understanding and applying these frameworks—utilitarianism, deontological ethics, virtue ethics, ethical relativism, justice theory, and care ethics—leaders can make informed choices that uphold moral principles and promote trust and integrity within their organizations.

Corporate Social Responsibility:

Introduction

Corporate Social Responsibility (CSR) has become a central business focus as stakeholders increasingly demand ethical practices and sustainable actions. Leaders are critical in driving CSR initiatives and ensuring their organizations contribute positively to society and the environment. This discussion explores how leaders can promote social and environmental responsibility within their organizations.

Setting a Vision for CSR

Leaders must articulate a clear and compelling vision for CSR that aligns with the company's values and strategic objectives. This vision should emphasize the importance of social and environmental responsibility and provide a framework for integrating these principles into the organization's operations and culture.

Example: Paul Polman, former CEO of Unilever, exemplified this by embedding sustainability into Unilever's core business strategy, committing to reduce the company's environmental footprint and enhance social impact through various initiatives.

Integrating CSR into Corporate Strategy

Influential leaders integrate CSR into the corporate strategy to ensure that social and environmental responsibility is critical to business decisions. This involves setting measurable goals, allocating resources, and creating policies that support sustainable practices and social contributions.

Example: Patagonia's leadership has embedded environmental responsibility into the company's strategy by committing to using sustainable materials and supporting environmental causes, which aligns with the company's mission and values.

Leading by Example

Leaders must model CSR values through their actions and decisions. By demonstrating commitment to social and environmental responsibility, leaders set a standard for employees and stakeholders, fostering a culture of ethical behavior and accountability.

Example: Starbucks' leadership, under Howard Schultz, has emphasized ethical sourcing of coffee and support for social causes, which has reinforced the company's reputation for social responsibility and influenced employee engagement.

Engaging Stakeholders

Leaders should actively engage with stakeholders, including employees, customers, investors, and communities, to understand their expectations and concerns regarding CSR. This engagement helps leaders to address issues effectively and build strong relationships based on trust and transparency.

Example: Ben & Jerry's actively engages with its customers and communities on social issues, using its platform to advocate for social justice and environmental causes. This fosters strong stakeholder relationships and enhances the company's brand reputation.

Promoting Transparency and Accountability

Transparency and accountability are essential for building trust and demonstrating genuine commitment to CSR. Leaders must ensure that their organizations are open about their CSR practices, report progress on sustainability goals, and address any challenges or shortcomings.

Example: Tesla's leadership has been transparent about the company's environmental impact and efforts to reduce carbon emissions through electric vehicles and renewable energy solutions, providing regular updates to stakeholders.

Encouraging Innovation for Sustainability

Leaders can drive innovation by supporting initiatives that focus on sustainability and social impact. This includes investing in research and development for environmentally friendly technologies and encouraging creative solutions that address social and environmental challenges.

Example: Google's leadership has promoted sustainability through investments in renewable energy and energy-efficient technologies, driving innovation in its products and operational practices.

Fostering a CSR-Oriented Culture

Creating a CSR-oriented culture involves embedding social and environmental responsibility into the organization's values, norms, and practices. Leaders play a crucial role in fostering this culture by recognizing and rewarding employees who contribute to CSR goals and integrating these principles into everyday business practices.

Example: Salesforce's leadership has integrated CSR into the company culture by encouraging employees to volunteer and aligning corporate practices with social responsibility goals, which has become a core aspect of the company's identity.

Addressing Global and Local Issues

Leaders must address global and local social and environmental issues relevant to their organizations. This involves understanding the broader impact of the company's operations and contributing to global challenges, such as climate change while supporting local communities and addressing specific regional needs.

Example: IKEA's leadership addresses global sustainability issues through initiatives like sourcing sustainable materials and reducing carbon emissions while supporting local communities through various social programs and partnerships.

Conclusion

Leaders play a pivotal role in promoting and implementing Corporate Social Responsibility by setting a vision, integrating CSR into strategy, leading by example, engaging stakeholders, and fostering a culture of accountability and innovation. By embracing these responsibilities, leaders can drive meaningful social and environmental impact and enhance their organization's reputation and long-term success.

Accountability and Transparency:

Introduction

Accountability and transparency are fundamental principles in leadership that foster trust, integrity, and effectiveness. Leaders who embody these principles enhance their credibility and create a positive organizational culture where ethical behavior and openness are valued. This discussion explores the significance of accountability and transparency in leadership roles and how they contribute to organizational success.

Building Trust and Credibility

Accountability and transparency are critical for building trust and credibility with stakeholders, including employees, customers, investors, and the public. When leaders are accountable for their actions and transparent about decisions, they demonstrate integrity and reliability, strengthening relationships and fostering confidence in their leadership.

Example: Satya Nadella, CEO of Microsoft, has emphasized transparency and accountability in his leadership approach. By openly communicating company strategies and being accountable for organizational changes, Nadella has cultivated a culture of trust within Microsoft.

Enhancing Decision-Making and Problem-Solving

Transparent communication and accountability contribute to better decision-making and problem-solving by providing clear insights into decision-making. When leaders are open about the factors influencing their decisions, stakeholders can understand the rationale, contributing to more informed and collaborative solutions.

Example: Paul Polman, former CEO of Unilever, demonstrated how transparency in decision-making can lead to positive outcomes. His open approach to sustainability challenges and goals allowed collaborative problem-solving and reinforced Unilever's commitment to ethical practices.

Promoting Ethical Behavior

Leaders who prioritize accountability and transparency set ethical behavior standards within their organizations. By holding themselves and others accountable for their actions and maintaining transparency in operations, leaders create an environment where ethical practices are encouraged, and deviations are addressed promptly.

Example: Howard Schultz, former CEO of Starbucks, implemented policies to ensure transparency and accountability in the company's supply chain. This approach improved ethical standards and enhanced the company's reputation for social responsibility.

Strengthening Organizational Culture

A culture of accountability and transparency fosters a positive work environment where employees feel valued and respected. Leaders who model these behaviors promote open communication, encourage feedback, and support employee engagement, contributing to a more inclusive and collaborative organizational culture.

Example: Google's leadership has fostered a culture of openness and accountability by implementing regular employee surveys and feedback mechanisms. This approach has helped address issues proactively and build a supportive workplace culture.

Managing Crisis and Recovery

Accountability and transparency are crucial during crises for managing the situation effectively and maintaining stakeholder trust. Leaders who are transparent about the nature of the crisis and accountable for their responses can navigate challenges more effectively and facilitate recovery efforts.

Example: New Zealand Prime Minister Jacinda Ardern's transparent and accountable communication during the COVID-19 pandemic demonstrated effective crisis management. Her clear updates and commitment to addressing public concerns helped maintain trust and support during a challenging time.

Driving Organizational Performance

Accountability and transparency can drive organizational performance by creating a culture of excellence and continuous improvement. When leaders are accountable for their goals and transparent about progress, they motivate teams to perform at their best and align efforts with organizational objectives.

Example: Salesforce's leadership practices transparency in performance metrics and goal-setting. This approach aligns the team's efforts with company goals and fosters a performance-driven culture that supports organizational success.

Enhancing Stakeholder Relations

Effective leadership involves managing relationships with various stakeholders, including customers, investors, and the community. By being accountable and transparent, leaders can build strong, positive relationships with stakeholders, leading to increased support and long-term success.

Example: Patagonia's leadership has maintained strong relationships with customers and stakeholders by being transparent about the company's environmental impact and sustainability efforts. This transparency has strengthened customer loyalty and supported the brand's mission.

Ensuring Compliance and Risk Management

Accountability and transparency are essential for ensuring compliance with legal and regulatory requirements and managing risks. Leaders who are transparent about their compliance efforts and accountable for risk management practices help safeguard their organizations against potential legal and financial issues.

Example: Johnson & Johnson's leadership has demonstrated transparency and accountability in handling product recalls and safety concerns. This proactive approach to risk management has helped the company maintain regulatory compliance and protect its reputation.

Conclusion

Accountability and transparency are vital principles in leadership that contribute to building trust, enhancing decision-making, promoting ethical behavior, and driving organizational performance. Leaders who embrace these principles foster a positive organizational culture, strengthen stakeholder relationships, and effectively manage crises and compliance issues. By prioritizing accountability and transparency, leaders can achieve long-term success and create a more ethical and practical organization.

7

Adapting to Rapid Change

Change Management:

Introduction

Leading through rapid change and uncertainty is a critical skill for modern leaders. Effective change management ensures organizations can navigate transitions smoothly, adapt to new conditions, and maintain productivity and morale. This discussion explores essential techniques for leading through change and uncertainty, providing a framework for managing transitions effectively.

Develop a Clear Vision

A clear vision for the future helps guide the organization through change and uncertainty. Leaders should articulate a compelling vision that outlines the direction and objectives of the change. This vision provides a sense of purpose and helps align the team with the new goals.

Example: Satya Nadella, Microsoft's CEO, provided a clear vision of transforming Microsoft into a cloud-first company. This vision guided the organization through significant changes and positioned it for long-term success.

Communicate Transparently

Open and honest communication is essential during times of change. Leaders should provide regular updates on the progress of the change, address concerns, and clarify how the changes will impact the team. Transparent communication helps build trust and reduces uncertainty.

Example: During the COVID-19 pandemic, New Zealand Prime Minister Jacinda Ardern used transparent communication to inform the public about health measures and restrictions, building trust and compliance.

Involve Key Stakeholders

Engaging key stakeholders early in the change process helps ensure buy-in and support. Leaders should involve employees, customers, and other relevant parties in planning, implementing, gathering feedback, and addressing concerns to create a sense of ownership.

Example: Google involves employees in decision-making processes through surveys and feedback mechanisms, ensuring that changes align with their needs and fostering a collaborative environment.

Build a Resilient Culture

Creating a resilient organizational culture helps teams adapt to change and overcome challenges. Leaders should foster a culture that values flexibility, continuous learning, and problem-solving, preparing employees to navigate uncertainty effectively.

Example: IBM's leadership promotes a culture of resilience by encouraging continuous learning and innovation, helping employees adapt to technological changes and market shifts.

Provide Support and Resources

Leaders should provide the necessary resources and support to help employees adapt to change. This includes offering training, tools, and assistance to address challenges and build skills needed for new roles or processes.

Example: Salesforce provides comprehensive training and support resources to help employees transition to new technologies and processes and ensure they have the tools needed to succeed.

Monitor and Adjust

Effective change management involves monitoring the progress of the change and making adjustments as needed. Leaders should track key performance indicators, gather feedback, and be prepared to pivot or refine strategies based on real-time insights.

Example: Netflix's leadership continuously monitors user feedback and performance metrics to adjust its content strategy and technology, ensuring the company remains responsive to market demands.

Foster Emotional Intelligence

Leaders should use emotional intelligence to manage the human side of change. Understanding and addressing the emotional impact of change helps leaders support their teams, reduce resistance, and foster a positive transition experience.

Example: Howard Schultz of Starbucks demonstrated emotional intelligence by addressing employee concerns during organizational changes, supporting their needs, and maintaining morale.

Lead by Example

Leaders should model the behaviors and attitudes they want to see in their teams. Leading by example helps reinforce the desired culture and demonstrates a commitment to the change process, inspiring others to follow suit.

Example: Elon Musk's hands-on approach to leading Tesla through product development and manufacturing challenges serves as an example of leading by example, inspiring commitment and perseverance in the team.

Celebrate Milestones

Recognizing and celebrating milestones during the change process helps maintain motivation and reinforces progress. Leaders should acknowledge achievements and milestones to build momentum and encourage continued effort.

Example: Microsoft celebrated critical milestones in its transition to cloud computing, recognizing team achievements and reinforcing the strategic shift's success.

Evaluate and Learn

After implementing changes, leaders should conduct a thorough evaluation to assess what worked well and identify areas for improvement. Learning from the change process helps refine future change management strategies and contributes to continuous improvement.

Example: After a significant organizational restructuring, GE's leadership evaluated the outcomes and gathered feedback to refine their approach to future change initiatives, fostering a culture of continuous learning.

Conclusion

Leading through rapid change and uncertainty requires clear vision, transparent communication, stakeholder involvement, and support. By fostering resilience, monitoring progress, and leading by example, leaders can navigate transitions effectively and guide their organizations through challenging times. Embracing these techniques ensures that change is managed smoothly, maintaining organizational stability and fostering long-term success.

Resilience Building:

Resilience, the ability to adapt and thrive amidst adversity and challenges, is a critical quality for individuals and organizations. Building resilience helps maintain performance, recover from setbacks, and sustain growth in the face of difficulties. This discussion outlines practical strategies for developing personal and organizational resilience, providing a framework to enhance adaptability and strength.

Foster a Growth Mindset

Personal Resilience: Embrace challenges as opportunities for learning and growth. Individuals with a growth mindset view failures and setbacks as temporary and surmountable, focusing on continuous improvement and personal development.

Organizational Resilience: Cultivate a culture that encourages learning from mistakes and supports innovation. Organizations that foster a growth mindset are better equipped to adapt to changes and seize new opportunities.

Example: Google promotes a growth mindset through its "fail fast, fail forward" philosophy, encouraging employees to learn from experiments and iterate quickly.

Build Strong Relationships

Personal Resilience: Develop a support network of friends, family, and mentors who can provide guidance, encouragement, and assistance during challenging times. Individual, solid connections offer emotional support and practical help.

Organizational Resilience: Create a collaborative environment where team members support each other and share resources. Internal solid relationships enhance communication and teamwork, which are crucial during crises.

Example: The Mayo Clinic emphasizes teamwork and collaboration in its approach to patient care, which helps build a supportive and resilient organizational culture.

Enhance Problem-Solving Skills

Personal Resilience: Practice critical thinking and decision-making to improve problem-solving skills. Resilient individuals can analyze situations, develop solutions, and act decisively under pressure.

Organizational Resilience: Implement structured problem-solving processes and encourage employees to develop solutions independently. Effective problem-solving practices help organizations navigate complex challenges and minimize disruptions.

Example: IBM's "Design Thinking" approach fosters problem-solving by involving cross-functional teams in creative and collaborative solution development.

Personal Resilience: Engage in self-care practices that promote physical and mental health, such as regular exercise, healthy eating, and mindfulness. Maintaining well-being enhances overall resilience and the ability to cope with stress.

Organizational Resilience: Promote employee well-being through health programs, work-life balance initiatives, and stress management resources. A healthy workforce is more resilient and capable of handling workplace challenges.

Example: Johnson & Johnson provides comprehensive wellness programs to support employees' physical, emotional, and financial health, contributing to organizational resilience.

Cultivate Flexibility and Adaptability

Personal Resilience: Develop the ability to adapt to changing circumstances and be open to new approaches. Flexibility enables individuals to adjust their strategies and stay effective in dynamic environments.

Organizational Resilience: Implement agile practices and encourage adaptability within teams. Organizations that embrace flexibility can respond quickly to market changes and evolving conditions.

Example: Netflix's adaptability in content delivery and business model evolution demonstrates its ability to stay ahead in a rapidly changing industry.

Set Realistic Goals and Expectations

Personal Resilience: Establish achievable goals and manage expectations to avoid overwhelm. Breaking down larger objectives into smaller, manageable tasks helps maintain focus and motivation.

Organizational Resilience: Set clear, realistic team goals and monitor progress regularly. Managing expectations and celebrating milestones contribute to sustained motivation and performance.

Example: Microsoft uses OKRs (Objectives and Key Results) to set clear goals and track progress, helping teams stay aligned and resilient during changes.

Strengthen Leadership Skills

Personal Resilience: Develop leadership qualities such as confidence, decisiveness, and effective communication. Strong leadership skills help individuals navigate challenges and inspire others to persevere.

Organizational Resilience: Invest in leadership development programs to enhance the skills of managers and executives. Influential leaders guide organizations through crises and foster a resilient culture.

Example: The Center for Creative Leadership offers programs that enhance leadership skills and resilience, preparing leaders to handle complex challenges effectively.

Encourage Continuous Learning

Personal Resilience: Engage in lifelong learning to stay informed and adaptable. Continuous education and skill development help individuals remain relevant and resilient in their careers.

Organizational Resilience: Foster a culture of continuous learning and professional development. Providing training and development opportunities enables organizations to adapt and innovate.

Example: LinkedIn Learning provides employees access to various courses, promoting ongoing skill development and resilience.

Develop Effective Communication Skills

Personal Resilience: Practice clear and open communication to express needs, seek support, and address conflicts. Effective communication enhances personal resilience by building understanding and cooperation.

Organizational Resilience: Implement robust communication strategies to keep employees informed and engaged. Transparent and consistent communication helps organizations manage change and maintain trust.

Example: Salesforce uses a comprehensive internal communication platform to ensure all employees are informed and connected, enhancing organizational resilience.

Learning from Failure:

While often viewed negatively, failure is a powerful catalyst for personal and professional growth. Embracing setbacks as learning opportunities can lead to valuable insights, innovative solutions, and improved resilience. This approach emphasizes transforming failure into a stepping stone for success.

Reframe Failure as a Learning Experience

Perspective Shift: Begin by altering your perspective on failure. Rather than viewing setbacks as purely negative, consider them opportunities for learning and growth. This mindset shift allows you to focus on the lessons that can be extracted from the experience.

Actionable Steps:

Reflect on what went wrong. Identify key learnings.

Apply those insights to future endeavors.

This process helps you understand mistakes and avoid them in the future.

Example: Thomas Edison famously said, "I have not failed. I've just found 10,000 ways that won't work." His approach to failure led to groundbreaking innovations and a successful career.

Analyze and Understand the Root Causes

Root Cause Analysis: To effectively learn from failure, conduct a thorough analysis to identify the root causes of the setback. This involves examining processes, decisions, and external factors contributing to the failure.

Actionable Steps: Use tools like the "Five Whys" technique to investigate the causes of failure more deeply. Understanding these causes enables more informed decision-making and problem-solving in the future.

Example: After a failed product launch, a tech company might analyze customer feedback, market research, and design flaws to identify what went wrong and how to address these issues.

Cultivate Resilience Through Adaptation

Resilience Building: Develop resilience by adapting and overcoming challenges. Use setbacks as an opportunity to build mental and emotional strength, which will enhance your ability to handle future difficulties.

Actionable Steps: Set new goals, create action plans, and implement strategies to address weaknesses identified from the failure. Continuous adaptation fosters resilience and promotes long-term success.

Example: An entrepreneur who faces a failed business venture can adapt by refining their business model, learning from customer feedback, and trying a new approach with renewed determination.

Seek Feedback and Support

Feedback Gathering: Actively seek feedback from peers, mentors, and colleagues to gain different perspectives on the failure. Constructive criticism provides valuable insights that can guide improvement. **Actionable Steps:** Engage in open and honest discussions about what went wrong and how to improve. Use feedback to make necessary adjustments and enhance your approach.

Example: A project manager who encounters project delays might seek feedback from team members and stakeholders to identify areas for improvement and prevent similar issues in the future.

Embrace a Growth Mindset

Growth Mindset Adoption: Adopt a growth mindset by viewing challenges as opportunities for development rather than insurmountable obstacles. This mindset encourages continuous learning and improvement.

Actionable Steps: Emphasize the importance of effort, persistence, and adaptability. Encourage yourself and others to view failures as a natural learning process.

Example: Athletes often embrace a growth mindset, using losses as motivation to train harder and refine their skills, ultimately leading to improved performance.

Develop a Resilient Action Plan

Action Plan Creation: Create a resilient action plan to address the lessons learned from failure. This plan should outline specific steps and strategies for overcoming similar challenges in the future.

Actionable Steps: Set clear objectives, establish deadlines, and identify resources needed to implement the plan. Regularly review and adjust the plan based on new insights and experiences.

Example: After a failed marketing campaign, a company might develop an action plan that includes market research, targeted messaging, and performance metrics to ensure a more successful campaign next time.

Celebrate Progress and Success

Celebrate Achievements: Acknowledge and celebrate progress and successes that result from overcoming failure. Recognizing achievements boosts morale and reinforces the value of learning from setbacks.

Actionable Steps:

Share successes with your team. Reflect on the growth achieved.

Use positive reinforcement to motivate continued effort and resilience.

Example: A team that completes a project after overcoming initial challenges might celebrate by acknowledging individual contributions and collective achievements, fostering a positive and resilient team culture.

Conclusion

Learning from failure involves:

Reframing setbacks as learning opportunities. Analyzing root causes.

Cultivating resilience. Seeking feedback.

Adopting a growth mindset. Developing action plans.

Celebrating progress.

By embracing these strategies, individuals and organizations can transform setbacks into powerful drivers of growth and success, ultimately leading to more significant achievements and resilience.**Build and Maintain a Positive Attitude**

Personal Resilience: Cultivate a positive outlook and focus on strengths and successes. Maintaining a positive attitude helps individuals cope with adversity and stay motivated.

Organizational Resilience: Promote a positive organizational culture by recognizing achievements and celebrating successes. A positive environment supports resilience and employee engagement.

Example: Zappos fosters a positive work culture through employee recognition and a focus on customer service excellence, contributing to overall resilience.

Conclusion

Building personal and organizational resilience requires a combination of strategies that foster adaptability, support, and continuous growth. By implementing these techniques, individuals and organizations can enhance their ability to navigate challenges, maintain performance, and thrive in

8

The Future of Work and Leadership

Workplace Evolution:

The modern workplace is rapidly evolving, driven by trends such as remote work, the gig economy, and flexible work arrangements. These changes are reshaping how organizations operate and how employees interact with their work, offering opportunities and challenges.

Embrace the Remote Work Revolution

Adapt to Remote Work: The shift towards remote work transforms traditional office environments, enabling employees to work from various locations. This trend allows for greater flexibility and can enhance job satisfaction, though it also requires new approaches to managing and maintaining team cohesion.

Actionable Steps:

Implement digital tools for communication and collaboration. Establish clear remote work policies and expectations.

Provide support for creating effective home office setups.

Example: Companies like Twitter and Facebook have adopted permanent remote work policies, allowing employees to work from anywhere and enhancing work-life balance.

Navigate the Gig Economy

Leverage the Gig Economy: The rise of the gig economy reflects a growing preference for flexible, short-term job opportunities. This trend offers workers greater autonomy but challenges job stability and benefits. Organizations must adapt to this flexible workforce while managing engagement and consistency.

Actionable Steps:

Develop strategies for integrating gig workers into teams.

Offer flexible work arrangements and competitive compensation. Address legal and benefits considerations for gig employees.

Example: Uber and Airbnb have built their business models around gig workers, offering flexibility and access to a broad talent pool while managing the associated challenges.

Implement Flexible Work Arrangements

Adopt Flexible Work Arrangements: Flexible work arrangements, such as adjustable hours and job sharing, cater to diverse employee needs and improve work-life balance. This trend can enhance employee retention and attract top talent but requires careful management to balance flexibility with organizational goals.

Actionable Steps:

Create policies that support various flexible work options.

Communicate clearly with employees about expectations and performance. Monitor the impact of flexibility on productivity and team dynamics.

Example: Google offers flexible work hours and the option for job sharing, contributing to high employee satisfaction and productivity.

Adapt Leadership Practices

Evolve Leadership Practices: As workplace trends change, leaders must adapt their practices to effectively manage remote teams, gig workers, and flexible arrangements. This includes developing new communication strategies, fostering inclusivity, and supporting diverse work styles.

Actionable Steps:

Invest in leadership training focused on remote and flexible management. Encourage open communication and feedback from employees.

Promote a culture of trust and accountability.

Example: Remote work leaders at Microsoft have successfully implemented virtual team-building activities and regular check-ins to maintain engagement and productivity.

Conclusion

The evolution of the workplace involves:

Embracing remote work by adapting communication and support systems. Navigating the gig economy with strategies for integration and engagement. Implementing flexible work arrangements to enhance work-life balance.

Adapting leadership practices to manage diverse work styles effectively.

By embracing these trends and adapting to new workplace dynamics, organizations can foster a more flexible, inclusive, and productive work environment, ultimately leading to greater employee satisfaction and organizational success.

Leading Remote Teams:

Managing and motivating remote teams presents unique challenges and opportunities. Effective leadership in a virtual environment requires a strategic approach to communication, team cohesion, and performance management. Here's a guide to best practices for leading remote teams successfully:

Establish Clear Communication Channels

Effective Communication: Clear and consistent communication is crucial for remote teams. Utilize various digital tools and platforms to ensure team members can connect seamlessly. This includes video conferencing, instant messaging, and project management software.

Actionable Steps:

Set up regular virtual meetings to discuss progress, address issues, and provide feedback. Use collaborative tools like Slack or Microsoft Teams to facilitate real-time communication. Document and share meeting notes and key decisions to keep everyone informed.

Example: Teams at companies like GitHub rely on regular video calls and an array of communication tools to stay aligned and connected, ensuring everyone is on the same page despite geographical distances.

Foster Team Cohesion and Trust

Build Relationships: Cultivating a strong sense of team cohesion and trust is essential in a remote setting. Leaders should actively work to build relationships and create a sense of belonging among team members.

Actionable Steps:

Encourage informal interactions through virtual coffee breaks or social events. Recognize and celebrate team achievements to build camaraderie.

Facilitate team-building activities that are engaging and inclusive.

Example: Automattic, the company behind WordPress, organizes annual company retreats and virtual meetups to strengthen team bonds and foster a supportive remote work culture.

Set Clear Goals and Expectations

Goal Clarity: Remote work can blur lines of accountability, so it's vital to set clear goals and expectations. Ensure that all team members understand their roles, responsibilities, and performance objectives.

Actionable Steps:

Define specific, measurable goals and key performance indicators (KPIs) for each team member. Provide regular updates on progress and adjust goals as needed.

Use performance management tools to track and review achievements.

Example: Salesforce uses performance management systems to set clear targets and track progress, ensuring remote employees stay focused and aligned with organizational objectives.

Provide Ongoing Support and Development

Support and Training: Remote team members may need additional support and resources to succeed. Invest in ongoing training and professional development to help them grow and stay engaged.

Actionable Steps:

Offer virtual training sessions and workshops to develop skills. Provide access to online learning resources and tools.

Schedule one-on-one meetings to discuss career development and address any challenges.

Example: Remote workers at HubSpot benefit from a range of online training programs and career development opportunities that support their professional growth.

Emphasize Flexibility and Work-Life Balance

Work-Life Balance: Flexibility is one of the main advantages of remote work. Encourage team members to maintain a healthy work-life balance and accommodate their individual needs.

Actionable Steps:

Allow flexible working hours to accommodate different time zones and personal schedules. Promote practices that help employees manage stress and avoid burnout.

Support a culture where taking time off is encouraged and respected.

Example: Basecamp supports flexible work hours and encourages employees to set boundaries between work and personal life, contributing to a healthier and more productive remote work environment.

Implement Effective Performance Monitoring

Performance Tracking: While it's important to trust your team, monitoring performance helps ensure that goals are met and issues are addressed promptly.

Actionable Steps:

Use project management tools to track task completion and progress. Provide regular feedback and conduct performance reviews.

Address any performance issues or obstacles proactively.

Example: Asana provides managers with tools to track project progress and individual contributions, helping to ensure accountability and timely delivery of work.

Conclusion

Leading remote teams effectively involves:

Establishing clear communication channels. Fostering team cohesion and trust.

Setting clear goals and expectations. Providing ongoing support and development. Emphasizing flexibility and work-life balance.

Implementing effective performance monitoring.

By adopting these best practices, leaders can create a productive and motivated remote team, ultimately driving success and achieving organizational goals.

Future Workforce Skills:

As work evolves, future leaders and their teams must adapt to a rapidly changing environment. Here's an exploration of the critical skills and competencies that will be crucial for success in the future workforce:

Technological Literacy

Understanding Emerging Technologies: Leaders and their teams must be proficient in using and understanding emerging technologies such as artificial intelligence (AI), automation, and data analytics. Technological literacy will enable them to leverage these tools effectively to drive innovation and enhance productivity.

Actionable Steps:

Invest in training programs that focus on the latest technological advancements. Encourage continuous learning to stay updated on emerging tech trends.

Promote cross-functional teams that integrate technological expertise.

Example: Leaders at companies like Google are highly skilled in AI and data analytics, enabling them to drive advancements and maintain a competitive edge.

Adaptability and Flexibility

Navigating Change: Adapting to new situations and embracing change is critical as industries and job roles evolve. Future leaders and their teams must be flexible in adjusting strategies and approaches to meet shifting demands.

Actionable Steps:

Foster a culture that embraces change and encourages experimentation. Develop resilience training to help teams manage uncertainty and stress. Implement agile methodologies to respond swiftly to market changes.

Example: Spotify uses agile practices to remain adaptable, allowing their teams to pivot quickly in response to evolving industry trends.

Emotional Intelligence (EI)

Managing Emotions and Relationships: Emotional intelligence is vital for effective leadership and collaboration. It involves self-awareness, empathy, and the ability to manage interpersonal relationships constructively.

Actionable Steps:

Provide EI training to enhance self-awareness and emotional regulation. Encourage practices that build empathy and strong interpersonal connections. Use EI assessments to identify areas for improvement and track progress.

Example: Leaders at organizations like Microsoft prioritize EI to foster a collaborative work environment and enhance team dynamics.

Critical Thinking and Problem-Solving

Analyzing Complex Issues: Future leaders need strong critical thinking and problem-solving skills to navigate complex challenges and make informed decisions. These skills help analyze data, evaluate options, and implement effective solutions.

Actionable Steps:

Promote activities and training that enhance analytical and problem-solving abilities. Encourage a questioning mindset and the use of structured problem-solving techniques. Support decision-making processes with data-driven insights and collaborative input.

Example: IBM's leadership development programs focus on cultivating critical thinking to address complex business challenges and drive strategic initiatives.

Global and Cultural Awareness

Understanding Diversity: In a globalized world, leaders must work with diverse teams and understand different cultural perspectives. This competency enhances collaboration and drives innovation by leveraging various viewpoints.

Actionable Steps:

Provide cultural competence training to improve global communication and understanding. Promote diversity and inclusion initiatives within the organization.

Encourage cross-cultural experiences and international collaborations.

Example: Unilever's leadership emphasizes global and cultural awareness to effectively manage its diverse workforce and international market presence.

Communication Skills

Effective Interaction: Clear and effective communication is essential for leadership and team success. This includes verbal, non-verbal, and written communication skills, which are critical for conveying ideas, providing feedback, and facilitating collaboration.

Actionable Steps:

Offer communication skills training and workshops.

Implement feedback mechanisms to improve communication practices continuously.

Use technology to enhance communication and information sharing within teams.

Example: Salesforce leaders excel at communication, using various platforms to engage effectively with their teams and stakeholders.

Innovation and Creativity

Driving Change: Innovation and creativity are crucial for staying ahead in a competitive landscape. Leaders and their teams should be encouraged to think outside the box and develop novel solutions to drive progress and growth.

Actionable Steps:

Create an environment that supports creative thinking and risk-taking. Provide resources and support for innovation initiatives and projects. Acknowledge and reward innovative contributions and ideas.

Example: Tesla's leadership fosters a culture of innovation, enabling their teams to develop groundbreaking technologies and solutions.

Collaboration and Teamwork

Working Together: Effective collaboration and teamwork are essential for achieving organizational goals. Leaders must be skilled in fostering a collaborative environment and ensuring that team members work together seamlessly.

Actionable Steps:

Facilitate team-building activities and collaborative projects.

Use collaboration tools and platforms to enhance team interactions. Develop strategies for managing and resolving conflicts constructively.

Example: Atlassian promotes teamwork through collaborative tools and practices that enhance team coordination and productivity.

Strategic Thinking

Long-Term Planning: Leaders must think strategically to plan and execute long-term goals and initiatives. This involves setting a vision, identifying opportunities, and aligning resources to achieve desired outcomes.

Actionable Steps:

Engage in strategic planning sessions and scenario analysis.

Develop skills in forecasting and trend analysis to inform strategic decisions. Align team objectives with the broader organizational strategy.

Example: Apple's leadership employs strategic thinking to drive product innovation and market positioning, maintaining its competitive advantage.

Ethical Leadership

Upholding Values: Ethical leadership involves making decisions that align with core values and principles. Leaders must demonstrate integrity, transparency, and responsibility in their actions and decisions.

Actionable Steps:

Establish and communicate a clear code of ethics and conduct. Provide ethics training and support for navigating ethical dilemmas.

Promote a culture of accountability and transparency within the organization.

Example: Patagonia's leadership is known for its ethical approach to business, focusing on sustainability and social responsibility.

Conclusion

Future workforce skills for leaders and their teams encompass: Technological literacy.

Adaptability and flexibility. Emotional intelligence.

Critical thinking and problem-solving.

Global and cultural awareness. Communication skills.

Innovation and creativity. Collaboration and teamwork. Strategic thinking.

Ethical leadership.

By developing these competencies, future leaders can effectively navigate the evolving landscape and drive success in their organizations.

9

Leadership Development and Lifelong Learning

Continuous Learning:

Continuous learning and self-improvement are crucial for future leaders in a rapidly changing world. Embracing a mindset of life-long learning ensures that leaders remain relevant, adapt to new challenges, and drive organizational success. Here's a detailed exploration of the significance of continuous learning for leadership development:

Staying Current with Industry Trends

Adapting to Change: Industries are evolving at an unprecedented pace due to technological advancements, market shifts, and new business models. Leaders must stay informed about these changes to make strategic decisions and maintain a competitive edge.

Actionable Steps:

Engage in regular professional development and training programs.

Subscribe to industry journals, attend conferences, and participate in webinars. Join professional networks and forums to exchange knowledge and insights.

Example: Leaders at tech companies like Microsoft and Google continually update their skills and knowledge to stay ahead of technological advancements and industry trends.

Enhancing Problem-Solving Skills

Improving Decision-Making: Continuous learning fosters the development of critical thinking and problem-solving skills. Leaders can approach challenges with innovative solutions and effective strategies by acquiring new knowledge and perspectives.

Actionable Steps:

Take courses or workshops focused on problem-solving and critical thinking. Apply new techniques and methodologies to real-world problems.

Encourage team members to share diverse viewpoints and solutions.

Example: Elon Musk's diverse knowledge base across multiple industries allows him to tackle complex problems and drive innovative solutions at companies like Tesla and SpaceX.

Cultivating Personal Growth

Developing Self-Awareness: Continuous learning promotes personal growth by encouraging self-reflection and self-improvement. Leaders who invest in personal development can better understand their strengths and weaknesses and work on areas that need enhancement.

Actionable Steps:

Seek feedback from mentors, peers, and team members. Set personal development goals and track progress.

Explore coaching and mentoring opportunities for guidance.

Example: Oprah Winfrey's commitment to personal growth through various learning experiences has helped her remain a dynamic and influential leader in media and philanthropy.

Building Adaptive Leadership

Embracing Flexibility: As the business environment becomes more dynamic, leaders must be adaptable and open to new ways of thinking. Continuous learning enables leaders to remain flexible and responsive to change.

Actionable Steps:

Participate in cross-functional projects and teams to gain diverse experiences.

Experiment with new approaches and strategies in different scenarios. Develop a growth mindset that embraces change and continuous improvement.

Example: Satya Nadella's leadership at Microsoft has been characterized by focusing on adaptive strategies and fostering a growth mindset among employees.

Expanding Leadership Capabilities

Broadening Skill Sets: Continuous learning helps leaders expand their skill sets beyond their expertise. This includes acquiring new competencies related to emerging technologies, leadership practices, and organizational management.

Actionable Steps:

Pursue advanced education, certifications, or degrees in relevant fields. Engage in interdisciplinary learning to gain a broader perspective.

Attend leadership development programs to enhance managerial skills.

Example: Indra Nooyi's pursuit of advanced education and continuous learning contributed to her successful tenure as CEO of PepsiCo, where she led the company through significant transformations.

Fostering Innovation and Creativity

Driving Innovation: Leaders committed to continuous learning are more likely to foster a culture of innovation within their organizations. Leaders can drive creativity and encourage innovative thinking among their teams by staying curious and open to new ideas.

Actionable Steps:

Create an environment that supports experimentation and creative thinking. Encourage team members to engage in learning activities that inspire new ideas. Invest in research and development to explore new possibilities and solutions.

Example: Jeff Bezos's emphasis on continuous learning and experimentation has been critical to Amazon's success as a leader in e-commerce and technology innovation.

Strengthening Team Development

Empowering Others: Leaders who prioritize their learning can better support and develop their teams. Leaders can inspire their teams to pursue their growth and development by modeling a commitment to education and improvement.

Actionable Steps:

Offer training and development opportunities for team members. Provide mentorship and coaching to help others achieve their potential.

Recognize and reward continuous learning and personal development within the team.

Example: Sheryl Sandberg's focus on personal and professional development has empowered her Facebook team to grow and achieve their goals.

Conclusion

Continuous learning is essential for future leaders to:

Stay current with industry trends. Enhance problem-solving skills. Cultivate personal growth.

Build adaptive leadership.

Expand leadership capabilities. Foster innovation and creativity.

Strengthen team development.

By embracing ongoing education and self-improvement, leaders can effectively navigate the complexities of the modern world, drive organizational success, and inspire their teams to achieve their full potential.

Mentorship and Coaching:

Mentorship and coaching are essential components of leadership development, providing emerging leaders with the guidance, feedback, and support needed to navigate their career paths and enhance their leadership skills. These practices foster personal and professional growth by facilitating learning, reflection, and skill-building. Here's a closer look at how mentorship and coaching contribute to leadership development:

Guidance and Support

Mentorship involves a more experienced leader (mentor) providing advice, wisdom, and support to a less skilled individual (mentee). Mentors share their experiences, offer insights into leadership challenges, and help mentees navigate their career paths.

Coaching: Coaching focuses on specific skill development and performance improvement. A coach works with the individual to set goals, develop action plans, and address performance issues. It is often more structured and goal-oriented than mentorship.

Actionable Steps:

For Mentors and Coaches: Establish clear objectives and expectations for the relationship. Schedule regular meetings and provide constructive feedback.

For Mentees and Coachees: Be proactive in seeking guidance, setting goals, and implementing feedback.

Example: An executive mentor at a tech company might guide a junior manager through the complexities of leading a team and navigating organizational politics, helping the manager prepare for future leadership roles.

Skill Development

Leadership Skills: Mentorship and coaching are instrumental in developing essential leadership skills such as decision-making, communication, and strategic thinking. They provide opportunities for practice and refinement of these skills in real-world contexts.

Actionable Steps:

For Mentors and Coaches: Focus on developing specific skills by setting targeted goals and providing resources or exercises that address skill gaps.

For Mentees and Coachees: Actively engage in skill-building activities and apply feedback to improve competencies.

Example: A leadership coach might work with an emerging leader to enhance their public speaking skills by providing practice opportunities and feedback, leading to more effective presentations and communication.

Personal and Professional Growth

Self-Awareness: Mentorship and coaching help individuals gain insights into their strengths, weaknesses, and leadership styles. This increased self-awareness is crucial for personal growth and effective leadership.

Actionable Steps:

For Mentors and Coaches: Encourage self-reflection and provide honest, constructive feedback to help individuals understand their personal development needs.

For Mentees and Coachees: Reflect on feedback and experiences to identify areas for growth and development.

Example: A mentor might help leaders identify and address their leadership blind spots, leading to greater self-awareness and more effective interactions with their team.

Career Advancement

Career Pathways: Mentorship and coaching support career development by providing guidance on career planning, skill acquisition, and navigating organizational dynamics. This support can help individuals advance their careers and achieve their professional goals.

Actionable Steps:

For Mentors and Coaches: Assist individuals in setting career goals, developing action plans, and preparing for advancement opportunities.

For Mentees and Coachees: Communicate career aspirations and actively work towards achieving set goals with the support provided.

Example: A career coach might help an aspiring leader develop a strategic career-advancing plan that includes identifying potential opportunities, networking strategies, and skill development.

Building Confidence

Confidence Boost: Mentorship and coaching help individuals build confidence by providing reassurance, positive reinforcement, and validation of their abilities. Increased confidence enhances leadership effectiveness and decision-making.

Actionable Steps:

For Mentors and Coaches: Recognize achievements, provide positive feedback, and support individuals in taking on new challenges.

For Mentees and Coachees: Embrace feedback, celebrate successes, and use positive reinforcement to bolster confidence.

Example: A mentor might help a new leader gain confidence by acknowledging their successes and encouraging them to take on challenging projects. This would lead to increased self-assurance and leadership capabilities.

Networking and Relationships

Professional Networks: Mentorship and coaching often involve expanding professional networks and building relationships with other leaders and industry experts. These connections can provide valuable resources and opportunities.

Actionable Steps:

For Mentors and Coaches: Facilitate introductions and networking opportunities to help individuals expand their professional connections.

For Mentees and Coachees: Engage in networking activities and leverage new connections to enhance career development.

Example: A mentor might introduce a mentee to key industry contacts, providing access to valuable resources and opportunities that can aid in career growth and development.

Feedback and Reflection

Continuous Improvement: Regular feedback and reflection are vital to mentorship and coaching. They help individuals understand their progress, identify areas for improvement, and make necessary adjustments.

Actionable Steps:

For Mentors and Coaches: Provide timely, specific feedback and encourage regular reflection on performance and development.

For Mentees and Coachees: Actively seek and reflect on feedback to make informed improvements and adjustments.

Example: A coach might conduct regular performance reviews with coachees, providing actionable feedback and encouraging reflection to guide ongoing development and success.

Conclusion

Mentorship and coaching play a crucial role in leadership development by:

Providing guidance and support. Fostering skill development.

Enhancing personal and professional growth. Supporting career advancement.

Building confidence.

Expanding professional networks. Facilitating feedback and reflection.

By implementing these strategies, organizations can effectively nurture and develop future leaders, preparing them to excel and drive success within their teams and organizations.

Developing Future Leaders:

Preparing the next generation of leaders is crucial for ensuring sustained success and innovation within organizations and societies. Effective leadership development involves fostering skills, mindset, and experiences that will equip emerging leaders to navigate complex challenges and drive positive change. Here are critical strategies for nurturing and preparing future leaders:

Cultivate a Growth Mindset

Emphasize Learning and Adaptability: Encouraging a growth mindset helps future leaders view challenges as opportunities for learning and development rather than obstacles. This mindset fosters resilience, creativity, and a willingness to embrace change.

Actionable Steps:

Promote a culture that values continuous learning and experimentation.

Provide resources and training to develop problem-solving and critical thinking skills. Recognize and reward efforts and improvements, not just outcomes.

Example: Leaders at companies like Google and IBM encourage a growth mindset by supporting innovation labs and offering professional development programs that allow employees to explore new ideas and learn from failures.

Provide Mentorship and Coaching

Guidance and Support: Mentorship and coaching are essential for providing emerging leaders personalized guidance, feedback, and support. These relationships help future leaders gain insights into effective leadership practices and navigate their career paths.

Actionable Steps:

Pair emerging leaders with experienced mentors who can offer advice and share experiences. Implement coaching programs that focus on developing leadership skills and personal growth. Encourage regular one-on-one meetings to discuss progress, goals, and challenges.

Example: Organizations like the Center for Creative Leadership offer executive coaching and mentorship programs to help develop high-potential leaders and guide them through their leadership journey.

Foster Practical Experience

Hands-On Learning: Providing real-world experiences is crucial for developing practical leadership skills. Hands-on opportunities allow future leaders to apply theoretical knowledge, make decisions, and learn from successes and failures.

Actionable Steps:

Offer internships, rotational programs, and project-based assignments to provide practical experience. Encourage participation in leadership roles within team projects, committees, or volunteer initiatives.

Create simulation exercises and case studies to practice decision-making and problem-solving.

Example: Companies like General Electric (GE) use rotational leadership programs to expose emerging leaders to various business functions and challenges, preparing them for higher responsibilities.

Develop Emotional Intelligence

Enhance Interpersonal Skills: Emotional intelligence (EI) is critical for effective leadership. Developing EI helps future leaders understand and manage their emotions and build strong relationships with others.

Actionable Steps:

Provide training on self-awareness, empathy, and communication skills. Incorporate EI assessments and feedback into leadership development programs.

Encourage practices such as active listening and conflict resolution.

Example: Programs like the Emotional Intelligence Network offer training and workshops to help individuals enhance their EI skills, which are essential for leading diverse teams and managing complex relationships.

Promote Strategic Thinking

Big-Picture Perspective: Future leaders must develop strategic thinking skills to make informed decisions and plan for long-term success. Strategic thinking involves analyzing trends, anticipating challenges, and setting vision and goals.

Actionable Steps:

Include strategic planning exercises and simulations in leadership training.

Encourage leaders to participate in cross-functional projects to gain diverse perspectives. Offer workshops and courses on strategic management and foresight.

Example: Leadership development programs at organizations like McKinsey & Company emphasize strategic thinking through case studies and strategic initiatives that require leaders to address complex business challenges.

Encourage Ethical Leadership

Foster Integrity and Accountability: Ethical leadership is fundamental for building trust and credibility. Future leaders should be equipped to make ethical decisions and uphold integrity and accountability values.

Actionable Steps:

Integrate ethics training and discussions into leadership development programs. Provide case studies on ethical dilemmas and encourage debate and reflection. Establish clear codes of conduct and ethical guidelines for leaders.

Example: The Ethics & Compliance Initiative provides resources and training for developing ethical leadership practices, helping organizations embed integrity into their culture.

Build a Diverse Leadership Pipeline

Inclusive Development: Ensuring diversity in leadership development programs helps prepare future leaders to navigate and lead diverse teams. A diverse leadership pipeline brings varied perspectives and experiences that drive innovation and inclusivity.

Actionable Steps:

Implement initiatives to recruit and develop leaders from diverse backgrounds. Foster an inclusive culture that supports diverse leadership development.

Provide mentorship and networking opportunities for underrepresented groups.

Example: Organizations like Catalyst focus on advancing women and diverse leaders through targeted development programs and advocacy, helping to build a more inclusive leadership pipeline.

Encourage Networking and Collaboration

Expand Professional Connections: Networking and collaboration skills are crucial for future leaders to build relationships, leverage resources, and gain new insights. Encouraging these skills helps leaders connect with peers, mentors, and industry experts.

Actionable Steps:

Facilitate networking events, conferences, and industry gatherings for emerging leaders. Encourage participation in professional associations and collaborative projects.

Provide platforms for sharing knowledge and best practices with other leaders.

Example: The World Economic Forum hosts global events that bring together leaders from various sectors to collaborate on addressing global challenges, providing valuable networking opportunities for emerging leaders.

Embrace Technology and Innovation

Adapt to Technological Advances: Future leaders must leverage technology and drive innovation. Understanding and incorporating emerging technologies into leadership practices is essential for staying competitive.

Actionable Steps:

Provide training on digital tools, data analytics, and emerging technologies. Encourage experimentation and innovation within teams.

Stay updated on technology trends and their impact on leadership and business.

Example: The innovation labs at companies like Amazon and Tesla exemplify how leaders can integrate technology and foster a culture of continuous innovation to drive growth and success.

Support Personal Well-Being

Ensure Balance and Resilience: Future leaders should prioritize their well-being to maintain effectiveness and avoid burnout. Supporting personal well-being contributes to sustainable leadership and overall productivity.

Actionable Steps:

Promote work-life balance and wellness programs.

Encourage practices such as mindfulness, stress management, and regular exercise. Provide resources and support for mental health and personal development.

Example: The employee wellness programs at companies like Google and LinkedIn emphasize the importance of well-being, offering resources and support to help leaders maintain a healthy balance.

Conclusion

Developing future leaders involves: Cultivating a growth mindset.

Providing mentorship and coaching. Fostering practical experience.

Developing emotional intelligence. Promoting strategic thinking.

Encouraging ethical leadership. Building a diverse leadership pipeline.

Enhancing networking and collaboration skills. Embracing technology and innovation.

Supporting personal well-being.

By implementing these strategies, organizations can effectively nurture and prepare the next generation of leaders, equipping them with the skills and mindset needed to drive success and navigate future challenges.

10

Visionary Leadership: Shaping the Future

Creating a Vision:

Developing and communicating a compelling vision is a critical leadership skill that drives organizational direction and inspires team engagement. A clear, compelling vision provides purpose and motivation, helping to align efforts and foster a sense of shared goals. Here are techniques for crafting and communicating a vision that resonates and guides the future:

Define the Vision

Clarify Purpose and Goals: Start by defining the organization's or initiative's core purpose and long-term goals. This involves identifying the values, mission, and aspirations that will shape the vision.

Actionable Steps:

Reflect on Core Values: Identify the vision's fundamental values and principles.

Set Ambitious Goals: Establish clear, ambitious goals reflecting the desired future.

Example: A tech startup might define its vision as "Transforming the way people interact with technology by creating intuitive, user-centric solutions that enhance everyday life."

Involve Stakeholders

Engage Key Stakeholders: Include input from critical stakeholders, such as employees, customers, and partners, to ensure the vision resonates with those impacted by it. Engaging stakeholders helps to build buy-in and support.

Actionable Steps:

Conduct Surveys and Interviews: Gather feedback from stakeholders to understand their perspectives and aspirations.

Incorporate Feedback: Integrate relevant feedback into the vision to reflect a shared purpose.

Example: A nonprofit organization might involve community members in crafting a vision to address local needs and aspirations, ensuring the vision aligns with the community's values and goals.

Craft a Compelling Narrative

Develop a Vision Statement: Create a concise and inspiring vision statement articulating the desired future state. The statement should be memorable, aspirational, and emotionally engaging.

Actionable Steps:

Use Clear Language: Write the vision statement in simple, clear language that is easy to understand.

Incorporate Emotion: Craft the statement to evoke a sense of purpose and passion.

Example: A renewable energy company might craft a vision statement: "Empowering a sustainable future by pioneering innovative clean energy solutions that protect our planet."

Communicate the Vision Effectively

Utilize Multiple Channels: Communicate the vision through various channels to reach all relevant audiences. This includes meetings, written communications, social media, and organizational events.

Actionable Steps:

Create Communication Materials: Develop brochures, presentations, and digital content to share the vision.

Regular Updates: Provide regular updates on progress towards the vision to maintain engagement and motivation.

Example: A university might use campus events, newsletters, and social media to communicate its vision of becoming a global research and innovation leader.

Align Actions with the Vision

Integrate Vision into Strategy: Ensure that organizational strategies, goals, and initiatives are aligned with the vision. This alignment helps to translate the vision into actionable steps and measurable outcomes.

Actionable Steps:

Develop Strategic Plans: Create strategic plans that outline how the vision will be achieved.

Monitor Progress: Regularly assess progress towards the vision and adjust as needed.

Example: A healthcare organization might align its strategic initiatives with its vision of providing exceptional patient care by implementing new technologies and improving service delivery.

Inspire and Motivate

Lead by Example: Through your actions and decisions, demonstrate commitment to the vision. Leading by example helps inspire others and builds trust in the vision.

Actionable Steps:

Show Enthusiasm: Display genuine enthusiasm and commitment to the vision in all interactions.

Celebrate Successes: Recognize and celebrate milestones and achievements that contribute to the vision.

Example: To inspire employees and stakeholders, a CEO might actively participate in initiatives aligned with the company's vision, such as launching new products or engaging with customers.

Foster a Shared Vision

Build a Culture of Ownership: Encourage team members and stakeholders to take ownership of the vision by involving them in its implementation and recognizing their contributions.

Actionable Steps:

Encourage Participation: Invite team members to contribute ideas and solutions related to the vision.

Provide Recognition: Acknowledge and reward contributions that support the vision.

Example: A nonprofit might involve volunteers in planning and executing initiatives related to its vision, fostering a sense of shared ownership and commitment.

Adapt and Evolve

Remain Flexible: Be prepared to adapt the vision as circumstances change. A compelling vision should be dynamic and responsive to new opportunities and challenges.

Actionable Steps:

Review and Revise: Regularly review the vision and make revisions based on feedback and changing conditions.

Stay Informed: Keep abreast of industry trends and developments that may impact the vision.

Example: To stay relevant and competitive, a technology company might adjust its vision to incorporate emerging trends, such as artificial intelligence and sustainability.

Conclusion

Creating and communicating a compelling vision involves:

Defining the vision with clarity and purpose.

Involving stakeholders to ensure alignment and support. Crafting a memorable and inspiring vision statement.

Utilizing multiple channels to communicate the vision effectively. Aligning actions and strategies with the vision.

Leading by example and inspiring others. Fostering a culture of shared ownership. Remaining flexible and adapting to change.

By implementing these techniques, leaders can develop and communicate a vision that motivates, aligns efforts, and drives the organization toward a successful future.

Influencing Change: How to Inspire and Mobilize Others to Work Towards a Shared Vision

Influencing change is a crucial leadership skill that involves inspiring and mobilizing others to align with and actively pursue a shared vision. Effective change leadership requires communicating the vision clearly, engaging others, and fostering a sense of ownership and commitment. Here are critical strategies for influencing change and driving collective action:

Articulate a Clear Vision

Communicate with Clarity: Ensure everyone clearly articulates and understands the vision. A well-defined vision provides direction and helps others grasp the purpose and goals of the change initiative.

Actionable Steps:

Craft a Compelling Vision Statement: Develop a concise, inspiring vision statement that captures the essence of the change.

Use Simple Language: Avoid jargon and complexity to ensure the vision is easily understood.

Example: A company undergoing a digital transformation might articulate its vision as "Becoming a leader in digital innovation by leveraging cutting-edge technology to enhance customer experiences and drive growth."

Build Trust and Credibility

Establish Trust: Trust is essential for influencing change. Demonstrate credibility through your actions, decisions, and consistency.

Actionable Steps:

Lead by Example: Exhibit the behaviors and values you expect from others.

Be Transparent: Communicate openly about the change process, including challenges and progress.

Example: A leader in a nonprofit organization might build trust by openly discussing the challenges of a new fundraising strategy and actively seeking input from the team.

Engage and Involve Others

Foster Engagement: Involve key stakeholders and team members in the change process to build engagement and commitment. Participation increases buy-in and helps identify potential challenges early.

Actionable Steps:

Create Opportunities for Input: Hold meetings, workshops, and brainstorming sessions to gather feedback and ideas.

Empower Team Members: Delegate responsibilities and involve others in decision-making.

Example: During a significant organizational restructuring, a leader might form cross-functional teams to develop and implement the new structure, ensuring team members have a say in the process.

Inspire and Motivate

Motivate Through Inspiration: Inspire others by connecting the vision to their values and goals. Demonstrating the benefits and positive impact of the change can increase motivation.

Actionable Steps:

Share Success Stories: Highlight examples of how the change has already positively impacted or will benefit individuals and the organization.

Recognize Contributions: Acknowledge and celebrate efforts and achievements related to the change.

Example: A leader implementing a new wellness program might share success stories of employees who have benefited from the program, thereby motivating others to participate.

Create a Sense of Urgency

Generate Momentum: Establish a sense of urgency to encourage immediate action and prevent complacency. Emphasize the need for change and the risks of inaction.

Actionable Steps:

Communicate the Risks of Delay: Clearly outline the potential consequences of not addressing the need for change.

Set Short-Term Goals: Implement short-term milestones to build momentum and demonstrate progress.

Example: In response to declining market share, a CEO might create a sense of urgency by outlining the competitive risks and setting ambitious short-term targets to revitalize the company's strategy.

Provide Support and Resources

Offer Support: Ensure that individuals and teams have the necessary resources, training, and support to adapt to the change. Providing adequate support helps reduce resistance and enhances the effectiveness of the change initiative.

Actionable Steps:

Develop Training Programs: Offer training sessions and resources to help employees adapt to new processes or technologies.

Provide Access to Tools: Ensure that necessary tools and resources are available to facilitate the change.

Example: A company introducing new software might provide training sessions and ongoing technical support to help employees transition smoothly.

Address Resistance and Concerns

Manage Resistance: Anticipate and address resistance to change by understanding concerns and providing solutions. Effective change management involves acknowledging and mitigating resistance.

Actionable Steps:

Listen to Concerns: Actively listen to feedback and concerns from those affected by the change.

Provide Solutions: Offer solutions and address specific concerns to alleviate resistance.

Example: During a policy change, a leader might hold town hall meetings to address employee concerns and provide reassurance about the impact on their roles.

Monitor and Adjust

Evaluate Progress: Regularly monitor the progress of the change initiative and be prepared to make adjustments as needed. Ongoing evaluation helps ensure that the change is effective and sustainable.

Actionable Steps:

Track Key Metrics: Measure progress against established goals and metrics.

Adapt Strategies: Adjust strategies and tactics based on feedback and performance data.

Example: A project team implementing a new customer service approach might track customer satisfaction metrics and adjust the strategy based on feedback and results.

Promote a Culture of Continuous Improvement

Encourage Ongoing Improvement: Foster a culture that embraces continuous improvement and innovation. Encourage individuals to continuously seek ways to enhance processes and contribute to the vision.

Actionable Steps:

Encourage Feedback: Create channels for ongoing feedback and suggestions.

Support Experimentation: Encourage experimentation and the exploration of new ideas.

Example: A tech company might create innovation labs where employees can test new ideas and technologies, fostering a culture of continuous improvement and adaptation.

Celebrate Achievements

Recognize Success: Celebrate milestones and achievements related to the change initiative. Recognition helps reinforce the value of the change and motivates continued effort.

Actionable Steps:

Hold Celebrations: Organize events or activities to celebrate successes and acknowledge contributions. **Share Success Stories**: Publicly recognize individuals and teams that are significantly contributing to the change.

Example: After successfully launching a new product, a company might celebrate by recognizing the development team's efforts and highlighting the launch's positive impact.

Conclusion

Influencing change involves:

Articulating a clear vision. Building trust and credibility. Engaging and involving others. Inspiring and motivating.

Creating a sense of urgency. Providing support and resources. Addressing resistance and concerns. Monitoring and adjusting.

Promoting continuous improvement. Celebrating achievements.

By employing these strategies, leaders can effectively inspire and mobilize others towards a shared vision, driving successful change and achieving organizational goals.

Legacy and Impact: Reflecting on the Long-Term Influence of Visionary Leadership

Visionary leadership is characterized by the ability to foresee potential, inspire others, and drive transformative change. The legacy of visionary leaders often extends far beyond their tenure, shaping organizations, communities, and industries for generations. Reflecting on this long-term impact reveals how visionary leadership can create lasting value and influence.

Shaping Organizational Culture

Cultivating a Lasting Culture: Visionary leaders play a critical role in establishing and nurturing organizational culture. Their values, beliefs, and strategic direction often become embedded in the organizational fabric, influencing behaviors, attitudes, and practices long after they have left.

Actionable Steps:

Articulate Core Values: Clearly define and communicate core values that reflect the leader's vision.

Promote Cultural Integration: Ensure these values are integrated into daily operations, decision-making, and employee interactions.

For example, Steve Jobs' emphasis on innovation, design excellence, and customer experience at Apple created a culture that continues to drive the company's success and influence the tech industry.

Driving Sustainable Change

Implementing Transformational Initiatives: Visionary leaders often spearhead initiatives that result in significant, positive changes within their organizations or societies. These initiatives can address challenges, improve processes, or introduce groundbreaking innovations.

Actionable Steps:

Focus on Impactful Projects: Identify and lead projects with the potential for widespread, long-term impact.

Build Sustainable Practices: Ensure these initiatives are designed with sustainability and scalability.

Example: Nelson Mandela's leadership in ending apartheid and fostering reconciliation in South Africa created a foundation for democracy and social justice that continues to influence the nation's trajectory.

Inspiring Future Generations

Mentoring and Developing Talent: Visionary leaders often leave a lasting legacy by mentoring and developing future leaders. Their guidance and mentorship help shape the next generation of leaders, ensuring their vision and values continue influencing the future.

Actionable Steps:

Provide Mentorship: Actively mentor and support emerging leaders within the organization or community.

Foster Leadership Development: Create opportunities for others to grow and develop their leadership skills.

Example: Warren Buffett's mentorship and investment philosophy have influenced countless investors and business leaders, contributing to a legacy of financial wisdom and ethical investing.

Creating Lasting Innovations

Pioneering New Ideas: Visionary leaders often drive the development of innovative products, services, or processes that leave a lasting mark on their industries. These innovations can redefine markets, set new standards, and create enduring value.

Actionable Steps:

Encourage Innovation: Foster an environment that supports creativity and experimentation.

Protect and Develop Innovations: Invest in protecting intellectual property and developing successful innovations.

Example: Elon Musk's ventures, including Tesla and SpaceX, have pushed the boundaries of technology and sustainability, creating innovations likely to influence multiple industries for decades.

Building Resilient Organizations

Establishing Robust Systems: Visionary leaders often build resilient organizations that thrive amidst challenges. Their strategic foresight and adaptability help create organizations that can withstand economic downturns, technological disruptions, and other adversities.

Actionable Steps:

Develop Resilience Strategies: Implement strategies that enhance organizational flexibility and adaptability.

Encourage Agility: Promote a culture of agility and responsiveness to change.

Example: IBM's transformation under leaders like Lou Gerstner helped the company adapt from a hardware-centric business to a services and software company, ensuring long-term resilience in a rapidly evolving market.

Contributing to Societal Progress

Influencing Societal Change: Visionary leaders can contribute to broader societal progress beyond their immediate organizations. Their initiatives and advocacy can address social issues, drive policy changes, and improve communities.

Actionable Steps:

Engage in Social Advocacy: Take active roles in addressing societal challenges and advocating for positive change.

Collaborate with Communities: Work with communities and stakeholders to identify and address pressing social issues.

Example: Malala Yousafzai's advocacy for girls' education has profoundly impacted global education policies and inspired movements for gender equality worldwide.

Leaving a Tangible Legacy

Establishing Lasting Institutions: Visionary leaders often establish institutions, foundations, or endowments that carry forward their vision and values. These legacies can make a difference long after the leader's departure.

Actionable Steps:

Create Enduring Institutions: Establish organizations or foundations that align with your vision and values.

Ensure Sustainable Operations: Develop strategies for these institutions' long-term sustainability and impact.

Example: The Bill and Melinda Gates Foundation, established by Bill and Melinda Gates, focuses on global health, education, and poverty alleviation, leaving a legacy of philanthropy and social impact.

Conclusion

The long-term impact and legacy of visionary leadership encompass: Shaping organizational culture.

Driving sustainable change. Inspiring future generations. Creating lasting innovations.

Building resilient organizations. Contributing to societal progress. Leaving a tangible legacy.

By focusing on these areas, visionary leaders can create enduring value and influence beyond their tenure, shaping the future and leaving a meaningful legacy for future generations.

Afterword

As we conclude our exploration into the evolving leadership land-scape, it is clear that the future holds immense possibilities and challenges. The journey through the chapters of this book has illuminated the multifaceted dimensions of leadership, shedding light on the skills, qualities, and strategies necessary for leaders to navigate an ever-changing world.

Embracing Change and Innovation

The future of leadership is inextricably linked to rapid technological advancements, shifting global dynamics, and evolving expectations of diverse teams. Leaders of tomorrow will need to be adept at leveraging emerging technologies, fostering a culture of continuous learning, and embracing innovation with resilience and adaptability. The emphasis on lifelong learning and the ability to manage and integrate techno-logical advancements will be crucial in maintaining relevance and driving progress.

Fostering Empathy and Emotional Intelligence

In an increasingly complex world, the human element of leadership—empathy, emotional intelligence, and relationship-building—will be the cornerstone of effective leadership. Leaders who can connect with their teams personally, understand diverse perspectives, and inspire trust will be better positioned to lead with integrity and authenticity. Empathy and emotional intelligence cannot be overstated, as they will serve as the bedrock for fostering collaboration and driving organizational success.

Navigating Global Challenges

The global issues of climate change, international conflicts, and societal inequalities will demand visionary leadership that is both bold and compassionate. Leaders must tackle these challenges with strategic foresight, ethical decision-making, and a commitment to sustainability. Influencing and mobilizing others towards shared goals while maintaining accountability and transparency will be critical in addressing these pressing global issues.

Nurturing Future Leaders

As we look to the future, investing in developing the next generation of leaders is imperative. Mentorship, coaching, and creating opportunities for emerging talent will ensure a continuous pipeline of capable leaders ready to tackle future challenges. By fostering a culture of mentorship and providing guidance, current leaders can leave a lasting legacy of growth and empowerment for those who will lead in the years to come.

Creating a Lasting Legacy

The ultimate measure of leadership lies in its impact and legacy. Visionary leaders who inspire, innovate, and lead purposefully will leave an enduring mark on their organizations, communities, and beyond. Their legacy will be defined not only by the successes they achieve but also by the values they instill, the change they effect, and the lives they touch.

Final Thoughts

As we move forward into an uncertain yet promising future, the principles and strategies discussed in this book will guide those who aspire to lead with vision, integrity, and resilience. The future of leadership is not a static concept but a dynamic journey shaped by our actions, decisions, and aspirations. May this exploration inspire current and future leaders to embrace the challenges ahead with courage and creativity to cultivate a future marked by growth, collaboration, and meaningful impact.

Ultimately, the essence of outstanding leadership lies in our ability to adapt, innovate, and inspire—qualities that will define the leaders of tomorrow. As we continue to evolve, let us commit to leading purposefully, embracing change, and fostering a world where leadership creates lasting, positive change.

Thank you for joining me on this journey through the future of leadership. May it inspire you to lead with vision, empathy, and unwavering dedication to creating a better world.

Wayne E. Smith

About the Author

Wayne E. Smith, EdD ABD, is a distinguished figure in leadership development, emotional intelligence, storytelling, and personal growth. His work is deeply rooted in 'agape' leadership principles—a style that emphasizes nurturing teams with love and purpose. Smith has become an influential author, educator, and speaker, inspiring individuals and organizations to embrace agape leadership. This transformative approach has the power to build effective, compassionate, and purpose-driven teams, inspiring personal and professional growth.

Smith's educational journey reflects his relentless pursuit of knowledge and expertise in leadership and human development. He completed his doctoral studies at Northeastern University, earning an EdD (Doctor of Education) and ABD (All But Dissertation) degree. This solid academic foundation has equipped him with a profound understanding of educational and psychological principles, which he skillfully weaves into his work. Additionally, Smith is a certified Career Coach, further extending his ability to guide individuals on their professional journeys.

At the core of Smith's work is his groundbreaking book *Agape Leadership: Nurturing Teams with Love and Purpose*. In this book, Smith not only delves into the essence of agape leadership but also provides practical strategies for leaders to cultivate this style. These strategies empower leaders to create environments where team members feel valued, supported, and inspired to contribute their best.

Beyond his written works, Smith's leadership style has been shaped by over five decades of experience in radio, advertising, and television production. As a speaker and educator, his dynamic presentations seamlessly blend real-world experience with academic insights, bringing the concepts of agape leadership and emotional intelligence to life in an engaging and relatable way.

Wayne E. Smith's influence extends well beyond the written word and public speaking. Through his writings, teachings, and leadership, he has inspired countless individuals to embrace agape leadership to foster personal and professional growth. His unique combination of academic rigor, extensive practical experience, and heartfelt commitment to nurturing others through love and purpose has established him as a thought leader in leadership, communication, and personal development. Smith continues to leave an indelible mark on those who aspire to lead authentically, using the principles of agape leadership to create lasting, positive impacts within their teams and organizations.

www.ingramcontent.com/pod-product-compliance
Lightning Source LLC
Chambersburg PA
CBHW060032210326
41520CB00009B/1098